D0745676

Cowardy Custard

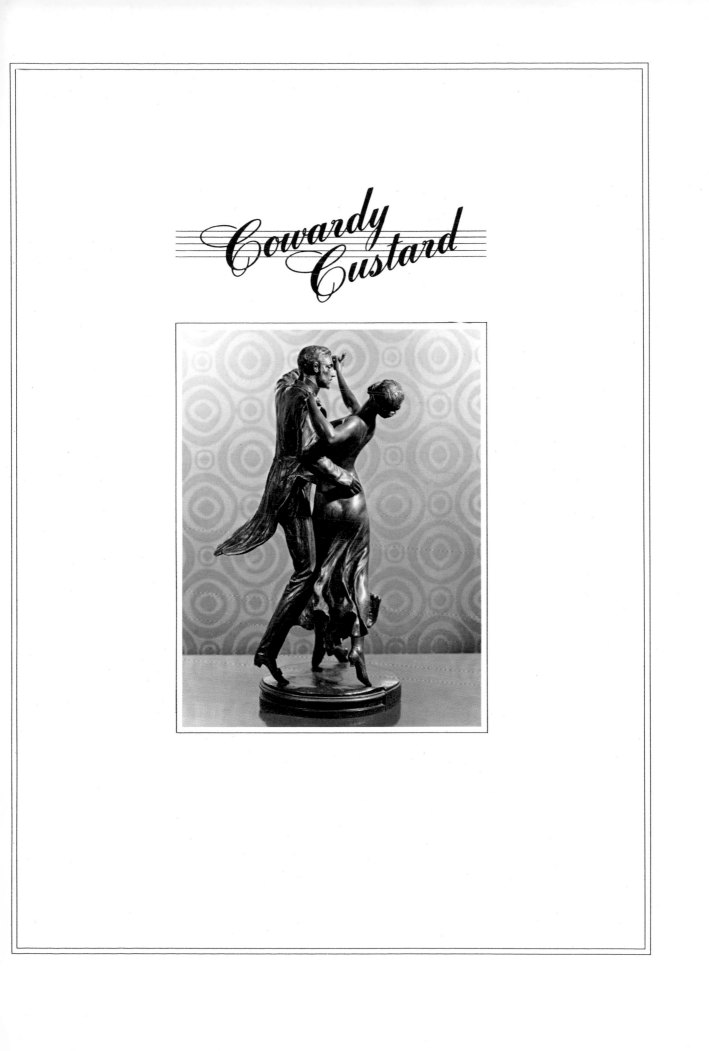

COWARDY CUSTARD

The World of Noël Coward

Edited by John Hadfield

Based on the

Mermaid Theatre Entertainment

devised by
Gerald Frow, Alan Strachan
and Wendy Toye

Heinemann
London

William Heinemann Limited,
London
Melbourne
Toronto
Johannesburg
Auckland

Designed and produced by
George Rainbird Limited
Marble Arch House
44 Edgware Road
London, W2

Picture research: ANNE-MARIE EHRLICH
Design: TREVOR VINCENT

First published 1973

© George Rainbird Ltd 1973

All rights reserved
This book, or parts thereof, may not
be reproduced in any form without
permission of the publisher

Printed and bound by
Jarrold & Sons Limited, Norwich
Colour plates and jacket originated and
printed by W. S. Cowell Limited, Ipswich

ISBN 434 310905

Half-title page colour plate:
'Tango', Art Déco bronze, by G. Eberlein
(By courtesy of Jonathan Morley, Esq)
Frontispiece colour plate:
Noël Coward, by Edward Seago
(By courtesy of the Phoenix Theatre, London)

BLUE HARBOUR
PORT MARIA
JAMAICA
WEST INDIES

13th March 1973.

Dear John Hadfield,

Thank you for everything. You
will I hope be pleased to know that I am delighted
by everything you sent and have no criticisms to
make, whatsoever.   Or suggestions; your approach
is so original and enjoyable that I feel sure the
result will be a lovely book quite unlike any other
- certainly unlike any other about my work, which
will be a relief and great pleasure for me.   I
am especially pleased with your Foreword; for me
to read such lovely, articulate and intelligent
praise is - I must use the same phrase - a relief
and great pleasure.   I quite see that you have had
to regroup the material, and like what you have
done and the titles you have chosen, especially
"This Blessed Plot".   Don't worry about any cuts
you may have to make, I am in fact rather pleased
that "Coconut Girl" may have to go - it is such an
out and out parody that it looks rather silly in
print I think.   Your treatment of "Alice" enchants

me - I wish I could help you over "Lousia" but I can't,
at the moment at any rate; if anything occurs to me I
shall let you know.   Do please let me know if you can
think of a way out of the dilemma, I should be fascin-
ated.

        Do please tell Mr Vincent how
very much I like his work.   And I do want you both
to feel free to carry on with the way you have started
- you don't have to turn to me over minor details.
I have complete confidence in you both.   My thanks
and my congrtulations.

        Yours sincerely,

Editor's Foreword

The enormous appeal of *Cowardy Custard* to audiences drawn from several generations of theatregoers is obvious proof of what Sir Noël Coward himself called 'a talent to amuse'. The lyrics and snatches of autobiography and dialogue which are brought together in this book form a triumphant reminder of the many forms of 'amusement' provided by this arch-entertainer of our times.

Yet the impact of Coward's lyrics and plays would not be what it is if they relied solely upon laughter and sentiment. It is a truism to say that he had a wonderful sense of timing. But his sense of timing went beyond that sense of an audience, that delicate manipulation of voice, words and melodies, which all great stage performers have. Sir Noël always had a more basic sense of timing than is provided by mere theatrical expertise. His writing, his acting, his *persona*, were always singularly attuned to the spirit of his age. They reflected the fashions, the follies, the moods and the sentiments of his world with uncommon clarity and accuracy.

The Young Idea, *Fallen Angels* and *The Vortex* epitomized the feverish re-shaping of social standards that followed World War I. 'Dance Little Lady' and 'Poor Little Rich Girl' are classic commentaries on the era of the Bright Young People. Following up the stylish sophistication of his songs and sketches for the Cochran revues with *Bitter-Sweet* showed a shrewd sense of the swing of public taste away from the rhythms of the Jazz Age to what might be called, to paraphrase Wordsworth, romance recollected in tranquillity.

One could continue to trace Coward's unfailing sense of mood and fashion, sentiment and taste, through three more decades. I myself can clearly recall the stunning impact of that celebration of traditional British values, *Cavalcade*, when it was produced just after Britain came off the gold standard and a few days before a disillusioned electorate returned a true-blue National Government. I can remember, too, the musical impact – and a much more subtle one than most people realized at the time – of 'London Pride' coming over the radio during the Blitz, and the intense poignancy – for someone who had himself been torpedoed in the Atlantic – of the closing scenes of *In Which We Serve*.

But I hope the point has been made. Noël Coward not only possessed a talent to amuse; he also happens to have been, throughout his career, a musical and dramatic sounding-box of public taste and emotion. His melodies, lyrics, sketches and plays reflect the changing social history of Britain and the United States through some fifty years as accurately as the plays of Congreve and Farquhar reflected the society of their times.

When, therefore, it was suggested that the 'book' of *Cowardy Custard* should be made literally into a book, and that the inevitable absence of the music (except in the inner ears of readers) should be compensated for by plenty of illustrations, it seemed to me that one might attempt to show visually how Noël Coward's lyrics have reflected the manners, popular sentiments and general *ethos* of his times.

Several admirable books have been published which illustrate the theatrical ambience of his work – the stage sets, the fellow-actors, the memorable performances. As a Coward archivist nobody could possibly compete with the encyclopaedic knowledge of Raymond Mander and Joe Mitchenson. What I have tried to do is to assemble a series of pictorial commentaries on the themes of some of Coward's lyrics and sketches. Instead of *Words and Music*, as he entitled one of his revues, this is a presentation of 'Words and Pictures'.

Noël Coward himself must in no way be held responsible for the choice of pictures. But I had hoped he would find some of them amusing, and some revealing, and some indeed, unexpected in the light they throw on his point of view. His death, whilst the book was 'in production', deprived me of the pleasure (as, generously, he led me to believe it would be) of his approval of the illustrations; but 'the show must go on', and here is the book.

The majority of the illustrations are news photographs, chosen from hundreds which have been culled from the archives of newspapers and press agencies by an indefatigable and imaginative picture researcher, Anne-Marie Ehrlich. To these have been added a few illustrations of paintings and other works of art which seem to me to be evocative of their period and the mood of Sir Noël's writing.

As editor of the book I am solely responsible for the choice of illustrations, though the design and layout of the book have been brilliantly carried out by Trevor Vincent. In case the nasty thought should occur to any reader that any of Sir Noël's lines or phrases refer specifically to any of the people shown in the photographs I must make it clear that this is not so. The photographs have been chosen solely as photographic images of the social climate, the kind of life which is reflected, in general terms even if often satirical terms, by Sir Noël's lyrics and sketches.

So here you have something that attempts to be a miniature off-beat history of our own times in pictorial terms. We have not had to commission anyone to write a text or a running commentary for it, since this is what Sir Noël had been quietly doing, in the guise of sheer entertainment, over the past fifty years.

I should mention that although the text of the book is based upon the miscellany of Sir Noël's lyrics and passages of dialogue and autobiography that was so brilliantly knit together for stage presentation by Gerald Frow, Alan Strachan and Wendy Toye I have altered the 'running order' and omitted a few of the items whose effectiveness depended essentially on stage presentation. And although in general I have tried to show how marvellously Sir Noël's writing reflected the 'period' quality of his times I have now and again for special reasons – as in the Seurat painting and 'Alice is at it again' – had to play a few tricks with time.   J.H.

A note by Sir Bernard Miles

The Mermaid Theatre began considering its contribution to the 1972 City of London Festival in the early summer of 1971. There were many different ideas for plays to celebrate the occasion, but the desire to offer something in a different vein to past presentations resulted in the decision to stage *Cowardy Custard*.

Coward's roots, for all his international success and cosmopolitan image, lie firmly in London. His autobiographies and poems recall with great affection and wit his upbringing in London's suburbs and his early days struggling to place his talent in the fiercely competitive London theatre of the 1920s. Musically too, London has always been a strong inspiration to Coward; songs such as 'London Pride', 'London at Night' and the 'London' song sequence from *The Girl Who Came to Supper* show him at his lyrical and musical best.

The show involved many months of preparation. Since Coward's output includes over fifty plays, musicals and operettas, at least 250 songs, not to mention sketches, his two autobiographies, plus the occasional poem, short story or novel, the main problem was obviously one of selection. Several early meetings with Raymond Mander and Joe Mitchenson, foremost among Coward authorities, provided a tremendous incentive for the research. Two of the show's devisers, Gerald Frow and Alan Strachan, were soon buried in the Coward archives in London, constantly surprised by new or forgotten material; and when Wendy Toye accepted the invitation to direct the production she added the experience of her previous work with Coward. The 1960s had seen the phenomenon of the 'Coward Revival' in his own lifetime ('Dad's Renaissance' as he called it himself), but his musical talent had been somewhat bypassed, and it is on this that the Mermaid's devisers concentrated. In the history of twentieth-century popular music only Cole Porter among other composer-lyricists has rivalled Coward's extraordinary range.

The songs in *Cowardy Custard* extend from the archetypal 'twenties Coward of 'Poor Little Rich Girl' and 'Dance, Little Lady', the romantic, lyrical mood of his C. B. Cochran musicals such as *Bitter-Sweet*, to the strong blues and jazz vein of 'Mad about the Boy' and 'Twentieth Century Blues', and of course the perennially inventive comic songs ('Marvellous Party', 'Nina', 'Mrs Worthington', etc).

The Mermaid gathered an impressive production team, including Tim Goodchild as designer, and John Burrows as musical Director. The orchestrations were by Keith Amos. The dazzling cast comprised Olivia Breeze, Geoffrey Burridge, Jonathan Cecil, Tudor Davies, Elaine Delmar, Laurel Ford, Peter Gale, John Moffatt, Patricia Routledge, Anna Sharkey, Una Stubbs and Derek Waring. Only one thing was missing shortly before rehearsals began – a suitable title. A telegram from Coward himself in Jamaica, suggesting *Cowardy Custard*, added the final ingredient, and a production initially intended for a limited eight-week season turned out to be one of the most successful shows in the Mermaid's history.

Drawing by Edward Burra

Programme

Colour Plates

Drawing by Edward Burra

Noël at the age of seven

Waldegrave Road

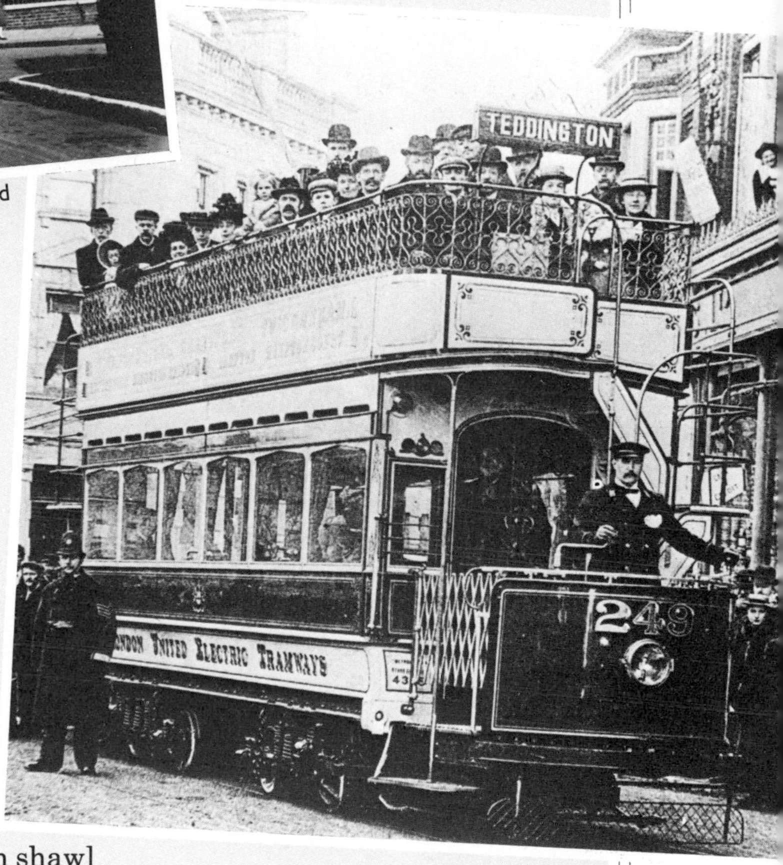

PERSONAL REMINISCENCE

I cannot remember
I cannot remember
The house where I was born
But I know it was in Waldegrave Road
Teddington, Middlesex
Not far from the border of Surrey
An unpretentious abode
Which, I believe,
Economy forced us to leave
In rather a hurry.
But I *can* remember my grandmother's Indian shawl
Which, although exotic to behold,
Felt cold.
Then there was a framed photograph in the hall
Of my father wearing a Norfolk jacket,
Holding a bicycle and a tennis racquet
And leaning against a wall
Looking tenacious and distinctly grim
As though he feared they'd be whisked away from him.
I can also remember with repulsive clarity
Appearing at a concert in aid of charity
At which I sang, not the 'Green Hill Far Away', that you know
But the one by Gounod . . .

Not Yet the Dodo, 1967

13

St Alban's Festival, Teddington

The social activities of Teddington swirled around St Alban's Church. It was an imposing building rearing high from the ground, secure in the possession of a copper roof which had turned bright green, and a militant vicar, the Reverend Mr Boyd, who was given to furious outbursts from the pulpit, in course of which his eyes flashed fire and his fingers pointed accusingly at old ladies in the congregation. He calmed down in after-years and became Vicar of St Paul's, Knightsbridge. Apart from him and the copper roof, the church's greatest asset was the Coward family, which was enormous, active, and fiercely musical.

Present Indicative, 1937

The Public Hall, Sutton:
scene of Master Noël Coward's first appearance on any public stage

In 1905 we moved to a small villa in Sutton, Surrey . . . I made my first public appearance at a prize-giving concert at the end of term. I was dressed in a white sailor suit and sang 'Coo' from *The Country Girl,* followed by a piping little song about the spring for which I accompanied myself on the piano. This feat brought down the house, and I had to repeat it.

Present Indicative, 1937

In *The Great Name* with Charles Hawtrey and Lydia Bilbrooke at the Prince of Wales' Theatre, 1911

THE BOY ACTOR

I can remember. I can remember.
The months of November and December
    Were filled for me with peculiar joys
So different from those of other boys,
    For other boys would be counting the days
Until end of term and holiday times
    But I was acting in Christmas plays
While they were taken to pantomimes.
    I didn't envy their Eton suits,
Their children's dances and Christmas trees.
    My life had wonderful substitutes
For such conventional treats as these.
    I didn't envy their country larks,
Their organized games in panelled halls;
    While they made snow-men in stately parks
I was counting the curtain calls.

As the Mushroom in the ballet *An Autumn Idyll*, with Joan Carroll, at the Savoy Theatre, 1912

I remember the auditions, the nerve-wracking auditions;
Darkened auditorium and empty, dusty stage,
Little girls in ballet-dresses practising 'positions'
Gentlemen with pince-nez asking you your age.
Hopefulness and nervousness struggling within you,
Dreading that familiar phrase, 'Thank you, dear, no more'.
Straining every muscle, every tendon, every sinew
To do your dance much better than you'd ever done before.
Think of your performance. Never mind the others,
Never mind the pianist; talent must prevail.
Never mind the baleful eyes of other children's mothers
Glaring from the corners and willing you to fail.

 I can remember. I can remember.
 The months of November and December
  Were more significant to me
 Than other months could ever be
  For they were the months of high romance
 When destiny waited on tip-toe,
  When every boy-actor stood a chance
 Of getting into a Christmas show.
  Not for me the dubious heaven
 Of being some prefect's protégé!
  Not for me the Second Eleven.
 For me, two performances a day.

Ah, those first rehearsals! Only very few lines:
Rushing home to mother, learning them by heart:
'Enter Left through window' – Dots to mark the cue-lines;
'Exit with the others' – Still, it *was* a part.
Opening performance; legs a bit unsteady,
Dedicated tension, shivers down my spine,
Powder, grease and eye-black, sticks of make-up ready
Leichner number three and number five and number nine.
World of strange enchantment, magic for a small boy
Dreaming of the future, reaching for the crown,
Rigid in the dressing-room, listening for the call-boy
'Overture Beginners – Everybody Down!'

Not Yet the Dodo, 1967

As Slightly in *Peter Pan* at the Duke of York's Theatre, 1913

🎼 PLAY, ORCHESTRA, PLAY

Play, Orchestra, play,
Play something light and sweet and gay,
For we must have music,
We must have music
To drive our fears away.
While our illusions swiftly fade for us
Let's have an orchestra score
In the confusions
The years have made for us,
Serenade for us,
Just once more.
Life needn't be grey,
Although it's changing day by day,
Though a few old dreams may decay,
Play, orchestra, play.

Listen to the strain
It plays once more for us,
There it is again,
The past in store for us.
Wake
In memory some forgotten song,
To break
The rhythm – driving us along
And make
Harmony again a last encore for us . . .

Sung by the Author and Gertrude Lawrence in
Tonight at 8.30: Shadow Play, 1935

Study for 'Le Chahut', by Georges Seurat
(Courtauld Institute Galleries, London)

Pierrot, 1918, by Pablo Picasso
(Metropolitan Museum of Art, New York. © by S.P.A.D.E.M., Paris, 1973)

♪ PARISIAN PIERROT

Fantasy in olden days
In varying and different ways
Was very much in vogue,
Columbine and Pantaloon,
A wistful Pierrot 'neath the moon,
And Harlequin a rogue.
Nowadays Parisians of leisure
Wake the echo of an old refrain,
Each some ragged effigy will treasure
For his pleasure,
Till the shadows of their story live again.

Mournfulness has always been
The keynote of a Pierrot scene,
When passion plays a part,
Pierrot in a tragic pose
Will kiss a faded silver rose
With sadness in his heart.
Some day soon he'll leave his tears behind him,
Comedy comes laughing down the street,
Columbine will fly to him
Admiring and desiring,
Laying love and adoration at his feet.

Parisian Pierrot,
Society's hero,
The Lord of a day,
The Rue de la Paix
Is under your sway,
The world may flatter
But what does that matter,
They'll never shatter
Your gloom profound,
Parisian Pierrot,
Your spirit's at zero,
Divinely forlorn,
With exquisite scorn
From sunset to dawn,
The limbo is calling,
Your star will be falling,
As soon as the clock goes round.

Sung by Gertrude Lawrence in
London Calling!, 1923

In between the matinee and evening performances the Coliseum stage had an even greater allure for me; with only a few working lights left on here and there, it appeared vaster and more mysterious, like an empty cathedral smelling faintly of dust. Sometimes the safety curtain was not lowered, and I used to stand down on the edge of the foot-lights singing shrilly into a shadowy auditorium. I also danced in the silence. Occasionally a cleaner appeared with a broom and pail, or a stage-hand walked across the stage, but they never paid any attention to me. An empty theatre is romantic, every actor knows the feeling of it: complete silence emphasized rather than broken by the dim traffic noises outside, apparently hundreds of miles away; the muffled hoot of a motor-horn and the thin reedy wail of a penny whistle being played to the gallery queue. As a rule there are a few exit lights left burning, casting blue shadows across the rows of empty seats.

THE LONDON COLISEUM AUDITORIUM.

THE MAGIC OF AN EMPTY THEATRE

Earl Carroll Theatre, New York

Present Indicative, 1937

AUDITIONS

In all theatrical experience I know of nothing more dispiriting than an average audition: a bleak, denuded stage only illuminated by one or two glaring working lights; a weary accompanist at a rickety upright piano; in the second or third row of the stalls, with the dim auditorium stretching behind them, sits a small group of people upon whom your livelihood depends, who mutter constantly to each other, and whose faces, on the rare occasions that they are turned towards the stage, register such forbidding boredom that gay words stick in the gullet, and voice-tones, so resonant in the bathroom, issue forth in strangulated squeaks. An additional horror is the awareness that the sides of the stage are packed with implacable ambition.

Present Indicative, 1937

♪ MRS WORTHINGTON DON'T PUT YOUR DAUGHTER ON THE STAGE

Regarding yours, dear Mrs Worthington,
Of Wednesday the 23rd,
Although your baby,
May be,
Keen on a stage career,
How can I make it clear,
That this is not a good idea.
For her to hope,
Dear Mrs Worthington,
Is on the face of it absurd,
Her personality
Is not in reality
Inviting enough,
Exciting enough
For this particular sphere.

Don't put your daughter on the stage,
  Mrs Worthington,
Don't put your daughter on the stage,
The profession is overcrowded
And the struggle's pretty tough
And admitting the fact
She's burning to act,
That isn't quite enough.
She has nice hands, to give the wretched
  girl her due,
But don't you think her bust is too
Developed for her age,
I repeat
Mrs Worthington,
Sweet
Mrs Worthington,
Don't put your daughter on the stage.

Don't put your daughter on the stage,
Mrs Worthington,
Don't put your daughter on the stage,
Though they said at the school of acting
She was lovely as Peer Gynt,
I'm afraid on the whole
An ingénue role
Would emphasize her squint.
She's a big girl, and though her teeth
    are fairly good
She's not the type I ever would
Be eager to engage,
No more buts,
Mrs Worthington,
NUTS,
Mrs Worthington,
Don't put your daughter on the stage.

Don't put your daughter on the stage,
    Mrs Worthington,
Don't put your daughter on the stage,
She's a bit of an ugly duckling
You must honestly confess,
And the width of her seat
Would surely defeat
Her chances of success,
It's a loud voice, and though it's not exactly flat,
She'll need a little more than that
To earn a living wage.
On my knees,
Mrs Worthington,
Please
Mrs Worthington,
Don't put your daughter on the stage.

Don't put your daughter on the stage,
    Mrs Worthington,
Don't put your daughter on the stage,
One look at her bandy legs should prove
She hasn't got a chance,
In addition to which
The son of a bitch
Can neither sing nor dance,
She's a *vile* girl and uglier than mortal sin,
One look at her has put me in
A tearing bloody rage,
That sufficed,
Mrs Worthington,
Christ!
Mrs Worthington,
Don't put your daughter on the stage.

Sung by the Author, 1935

26

NEW YORK, 1921

On my first visit to America in 1921 I got to know New York thoroughly, better actually than I have ever known it since. The subway, the elevated, cheap cafeterias, park benches and loneliness have been no part of my later visits. But I felt, even then, certain small regrets.

To be poor in your own country is bad enough, and to be poor among strangers should, by rights, be very much worse. But, somewhat to my surprise, I realized that in my case it had not been worse at all. I remembered the Chinese laundry-man, the Italian grocer and the Irish 'cop'. I remembered conversations in buses, and cinemas, and soda-fountains. I remembered the beauty of New York at night, viewed, not from a smart penthouse on Park Avenue, but from a crowded seat in Washington Square. And it seemed, in spite of its hardness and irritating, noisy efficiency, a great and exciting place.

Present Indicative, 1937

The New York Edison Company
Photographic Bureau

At Home: Our Most Daring Playwright.

Noël Coward with his Secretary, Lorn Loraine

SUCCESS

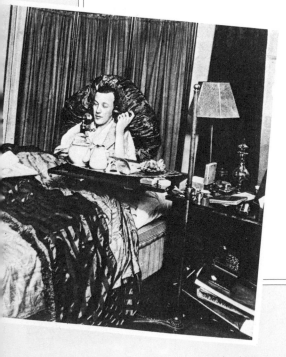

Success altered the face of London for me. Just for a little the atmosphere felt lighter. I'm not sure whether or not the people who passed me in the street appeared to be more smiling and gay than they had been hitherto, but I expect they did. I do know that very soon life began to feel over-crowded. Every minute of the day was occupied, and I relaxed, rather indiscriminately, into a welter of publicity. No Press interviewer, photographer, or gossip-writer had to fight in order to see me, I was wide open to them all; smiling and burbling bright witticisms, giving my views on this and that, discussing such problems as whether or not the modern girl would make a good mother, or what would be my ideal in a wife, etc. My opinion was asked for, and given, on current books and plays. I made a few adequately witty jokes

which were immediately misquoted or twisted round the wrong way, thereby denuding them of any humour they might originally have had. I was photographed in every conceivable position. Not only was *I* photographed, but my dressing room was photographed, my car was photographed, my rooms in Ebury Street were photographed. It was only by an oversight, I am sure, that our lodgers escaped the camera.

I took to wearing coloured turtle-necked jerseys, actually more for comfort than effect, and soon I was informed by my evening paper that I had started a fashion. I believe that to a certain extent this was really true; at any rate, during the ensuing months I noticed more and more of our seedier West End chorus boys parading about London in them.

Present Indicative, 1937

PENALTY OF SUCCESS

Garry Essendine	A drink?
Roland Maule	No thank you.
Garry	(*sitting*) Tell me – how old are you?
Roland	Twenty-five. Why?
Garry	It doesn't really matter. I just wondered.
Roland	How old are you?
Garry	Forty in December – Jupiter, you know – very energetic.
Roland	(*laughing, then serious*) Yes, of course. (*He has a nervous, braying laugh*)
Garry	So you've come all the way from Uckfield?
Roland	It isn't very far.
Garry	I know, but it sounds sort of far, doesn't it?
Roland	(*defensively*) It's quite near Lewes.
Garry	Oh, there's nothing to worry about then, is there?
	(*Enter Monica, Garry's secretary*)
Garry	Oh, Monica, I must introduce you. My secretary, Miss Reed – Mr Roland Maule.
Roland	(*shaking hands*) How do you do?
Monica	I have your script in the office if you'd like to take it with you.
Roland	Oh, thank you very much.
Monica	I'll put it in an envelope for you.
Roland	Yes.
	(*Exit Monica*)
Garry	Do sit down again, won't you? (*Roland sits*) Now, I must talk to you about your play.
Roland	(*gloomily*) I expect you hated it.
Garry	Well, to be candid, I did think it was a little uneven.
Roland	I thought you'd say that.
Garry	I'm glad I'm running so true to form.
Roland	Well, I mean, it really isn't the sort of thing you would like, is it?
Garry	In that case, why on earth did you send it to me?
Roland	I just took a chance. I mean I know you only play rather trashy stuff as a rule, but I thought you just might like to have a shot at something deeper.
Garry	What is there in your play, Mr Maule, that you consider so deep? Apart from the plot, which is completely submerged after the first four pages?
Roland	Plots aren't important, it's ideas that matter. (*pointing at Garry*) Look at Chekhov.
Garry	In addition to ideas I think we might concede Chekhov a certain flimsy sense of psychology, don't you?
Roland	You mean my play isn't psychologically accurate?
Garry	(*gently*) It isn't very good, you know, really it isn't.

Roland I think it's very good indeed.

Garry I understand that perfectly, but you must admit that my opinion, based on a lifelong experience of the theatre, might be the right one.

Roland (*contemptuously*) The commerical theatre.

Garry Oh dear, oh dear, oh dear!

Roland I suppose you'll say that Shakespeare wrote for the commercial theatre and that the only point of doing anything with the drama at all is to make money! All those old arguments. (*He points his finger*) What you don't realize is that the theatre of the future is the theatre of ideas. (*He taps his forehead*)

Garry That may be, but at the moment I am occupied with the theatre of the present. (*He taps his forehead*)

Roland (*rising, heatedly*) And what do you do with it? Every play you appear in is exactly the same – superficial, frivolous, without even the slightest intellectual significance. (*He points*) You have a great following and a strong personality and all you do is prostitute yourself every night of your life. All you do with your talent is wear dressing-gowns and make witty remarks when you might be really helping people, making them think! Making them feel! If you want to live in people's memories, to go down to posterity as an important man, you'd better do something about it quickly. There isn't a moment to be lost.

Garry (*rising*) I don't give a hoot about posterity. Why should I worry about what people think of me when I'm dead as a doornail anyway? My worst defect is that I am too apt to worry about what people think of me when I'm alive. But I'm not going to do that any more. I'm changing my methods and you're my first experiment. Sit down. (*He pushes Roland down on settee*) As a rule, when insufferable young beginners have the impertinence to criticize me, I dismiss the whole thing lightly because I'm embarrassed for them – and consider it not quite fair game to puncture their inflated egos too sharply. But this time, my highbrow young friend, you're going to get it in the neck. To begin with, your play isn't a play at all. It's a meaningless jumble of adolescent pseudo-intellectual poppycock. It bears no relation to the theatre or to life or to anything. And you yourself wouldn't be here at this moment if I hadn't been bloody fool enough to pick up the telephone when my secretary wasn't looking. Now that you are here, however, I would like to tell you this. If you wish to become a playwright, you leave the theatre of tomorrow to take care of itself. Go and get yourself a job as a butler in a repertory company, if they'll have you. Learn from the ground up how plays are constructed, what is actable and what isn't. Then sit down and write at least twenty plays one after the other, and if you can manage to get the twenty-first produced for a Sunday night performance, you'll be damned lucky!

Roland (*hypnotized*) I'd no idea you were like this! You're wonderful!

Garry (*flinging up his hands*) My God!

Roland I'm awfully sorry if you think I was impertinent just now, but I'm awfully glad too, because if I hadn't been you wouldn't have got angry, and if you hadn't got angry, I shouldn't have known what you're really like.

Garry You don't in the least know what I'm really like.

Roland Oh yes I do – now.

Garry I can't see that it matters anyway.

Roland It matters to me.

Garry How do you mean?

Roland Do you really want to know?

Garry What are you talking about?

Roland Well, it's rather difficult to explain.

Garry What is rather difficult to explain?

Roland What I feel about you.

Garry (*indicating door*) Now, my dear young man . . .

Roland No, no, no please. Let me speak. You see, in a way I've been rather unhappy about you, for quite a long time – you've been a sort of obsession with me. I saw you in your last play forty-seven times; one week I came every night, in the pit, because I was up in town trying to pass an exam.

Garry Did you pass it?

Roland No, I didn't.

Garry I'm not entirely surprised.

Roland (*rising*) My father wants me to be a lawyer. Ha! Imagine!

Garry Imagine!

Roland That's what the exam was for. But actually I've been studying psychology a great deal because somehow I felt that I wasn't at peace with myself. Then gradually, bit by bit, I began to realize that you signified something to me.

Garry What sort of something?

Roland I don't quite know – not yet.

Garry That 'not yet' is one of the most sinister remarks I've ever heard.

Roland Don't laugh at me, please. I'm always sick if anyone laughs at me.

Garry (*smiling behind his hand*) Forgive me, but you know, you really are the most peculiar young man.

Roland I'm all right now, though. I feel fine!

Garry I'm delighted to hear it.

Roland When can I come and see you again?

Garry I'm afraid you can't. You see, I'm going to Africa.

Roland Would you see me if I came to Africa too?

Garry I really think you'd be far happier in Uckfield.

Roland (*laughing and pointing*) I expect you think I'm mad, but I'm not a bit really. I just mind deeply about certain things. But I feel much better now because I think I shall be able to sublimate you all right.

Garry   Sublimate me?

Roland   Yes.

Garry   Then I'm afraid I shall have to ask you to go away and start now. (*looks at his watch, rising*) I'm expecting my manager, and we have some business to discuss.

Roland   (*rising*) Oh, that's all right. I'm going immediately.

Garry   Shall I get you your script?

Roland   Oh! No, no, tear it up – you were right about it. It was only written with a part of myself. I see that now. Goodbye.

Garry   Goodbye.

        (*Exit Roland*)

Garry   Monica! Monica!

        (*Enter Monica*)

Monica   Has he gone?

Garry   If that young man rings up again, get rid of him at all costs. He's mad as a hatter.

Monica   What did he do?

Garry   He started by insulting me, and ended up by sublimating me.

Monica   Poor dear, you look quite shattered.

Garry   I am.

Present Laughter, 1942

Noël Coward and James Donald
as Garry Essendine and Roland Maule
in *Present Laughter,* 1942

Let's Do It

♪ **TRY TO LEARN TO LOVE**

First you learn to spell
A little bit,
Then, if you excel
A little bit,
Other things as well
A little bit
Come your way;
Though the process may be slow to you
Knowledge of the world will flow to you,
Steadily you grow a little bit,
Day by day;
Though you're too gentle, sentimental,
In fact, quite a dreary bore,
Though you're aesthetic, apathetic
To all men but Bernard Shaw,
Use the velvet glove
A little bit,
Emulate the dove
A little bit,
Try to learn to love a little bit more.

First you droop your eyes
A little bit,
Then if you are wise
A little bit
Register surprise
A little bit,
If he's bold,
Stamp your foot with some celerity,
Murmur with intense sincerity
That his immature temerity
Leaves you cold.
But when you get him
You must let him
Have the joy he's yearning for
And whisper sweetly,
Indiscreetly,
He's the boy that you adore
Use the moon above
A little bit,
Emulate the dove
A little bit,
Try to learn to love – a little bit more.

Sung by Jessie Matthews and Sonnie Hale in
This Year of Grace!, 1928

♪ IN A BOAT,...
WITH MY DARLING

In a boat, on a lake, with my darling
In the heat of a sweet summer day,
There's the sound of the breeze
In the green willow trees
And the noise of the town fades away
Letting time flutter by like a starling
As we gaze into
The infinite blue
Above
Hand in hand,
Heart to heart,
Just a moment apart,
In a boat, on a lake, with my love.

Sung by Myles Eason and Jean Carson in
Ace of Clubs, 1950

♪ DEAREST LOVE

John I saw your face,
Shadows of the morning cleared,
I knew that suddenly
The world had dropped away.

Mary Somewhere in space
Some new lovely star appeared
To rule our destiny
For ever and a day.

John I knew, the moment that I touched your
hand,
The gods had planned
Our meeting.

Mary Now in this instant in the whole of Time
Our lovers' rhyme
Is near completing.

John I saw you turn away and for a while
My poor heart drooped and faltered;
And then I saw your strange elusive smile
And all my life was altered.

Both My dearest dear,
For evermore
The happiness we've waited for
At last is here . . .

Dearest Love,
Now that I've found you
The stars change in the sky,
Every song is new,
Every note is true,
Sorrows like the clouds go sailing by.
Here, my Love,
Magic has bound you
To me – ever to be
In my heart supreme,
Dearer than my dearest dream,
The only love for me!

Sung by Muriel Barron and Max Oldaker, and also by Peggy Wood, in *Operette*, 1938

ERICH AUERBACH

♪ YOU WERE THERE

Was it in the real world
Or was it in a dream?
Was it just a note from some eternal theme?
Was it accidental
Or accurately planned?
How could I hesitate
Knowing that my fate,
Led me by the hand?

You were there,
I saw you and my heart stopped beating,
You were there
And in that first enchanted meeting
Life changed its tune
The stars, the moon
Came near to me,
Dreams that I dreamed
Like magic seemed
To be clear to me, dear to me.
You were there,
Your eyes looked into mine and faltered.
Everywhere
The colour of the whole world altered.
False became true,
My universe tumbled in two,
The earth became heaven, for you
Were there.

Sung by the Author and Gertrude Lawrence in *Tonight at 8.30: Shadow Play*, 1935

🎼 A ROOM WITH A VIEW

He A room with a view – and you,
With no one to worry us,
No one to hurry us – through
This dream we've found,
We'll gaze at the sky – and try
To guess what it's all about,
Then we will figure out – why
The world is round.

She We'll be as happy and contented
As birds upon a tree,
High above the mountains and the sea.

Both We'll bill and we'll coo-oo-oo
And sorrow will never come,
Oh, will it ever come – true,
Our room with a view.

He We'll watch the whole world pass before us
While we are sitting still
Leaning on our own window-sill.

Both We'll bill and we'll coo-oo-oo,
And maybe a stork will bring
This, that and t'other thing – to
Our room with a view.

Sung by Sonnie Hale and Jessie Matthews in
This Year of Grace!, 1928

🎼 POOR LITTLE RICH GIRL

You're only
A baby,
You're lonely,
And maybe
Some day soon you'll know
The tears
You are tasting
Are years
You are wasting,
Life's a bitter foe,
With fate it's no use competing,
Youth is so terribly fleeting;
By dancing
Much faster,
You're chancing
Disaster,
Time alone will show.

Poor little rich girl,
You're a bewitched girl,
Better beware!
Laughing at danger,
Virtue a stranger,
Better take care!
The life you lead sets all your nerves a jangle,
Your love affairs are in a hopeless tangle,
Though you're a child, dear,
Your life's a wild typhoon,

In lives of leisure
The craze for pleasure
Steadily grows.
Cocktails and laughter,
But what comes after?
Nobody knows.
You're weaving love into a mad jazz pattern,
Ruled by Pantaloon.
Poor little rich girl, don't drop a stitch too soon.

The role you are acting,
The toll is exacting,
Soon you'll have to pay.
The music of living,
You lose in the giving,
False things soon decay.
These words from me may surprise you,
I've got no right to advise you,
I've known life too well, dear,
Your own life must tell, dear,
Please don't turn away.

Sung by Alice Delysia in *On With the Dance,* 1925

Girl with Red Hair, 1926, by Jules Pascin
(Private Collection. © by S.P.A.D.E.M., Paris, 1973)

Scene from 'The Modern Rake's Progress', 1934, by David Low
(By arrangement with the Trustees and the London Evening Standard)

47

Columbine and Harlequin: Art Déco sculpture by Prof. Otto Poertzel
(By courtesy of Bryan Catley, Esq.)

Though you're only seventeen
Far too much of life you've seen,
Syncopated child.
Maybe if you only knew
Where your path was leading to
You'd become less wild.
But I know it's vain
Trying to explain
While there's this insane
Music in your brain.

Dance, dance, dance little lady,
Youth is fleeting – to the rhythm beating
In your mind.
Dance, dance, dance little lady,
So obsessed with second best,
No rest you'll ever find,
Time and tide and trouble
Never, never wait.
Let the cauldron bubble
Justify your fate.
Dance, dance, dance little lady,
Leave tomorrow behind.

DANCE LITTLE LADY

Sung by Sonnie Hale and danced by Lauri Devine in *This Year of Grace*, 1928

Lauri Devine in *This Year of Grace!*: masks by Oliver Messel

𝄞 LET'S DO IT

(With acknowledgments to Cole Porter)

Mr Irving Berlin
Often emphasizes sin
In a charming way.
Mr Coward we know
Wrote a song or two to show
Sex was here to stay.
Richard Rogers it's true
Took a more romantic view
Of that sly biological urge.
But it really was Cole
Who contrived to make the whole
Thing merge.

He said that Belgians and Greeks do it,
Nice young men who sell antiques do it,
Let's do it, let's fall in love.
Monkeys when ever you look do it,
Rupert Bear and even Flook do it,
Let's do it, let's fall in love.
Mary Whitehouse can't quite do it
But she is so highly strung,
Marlene might do it
But she looks far too young,
Excited spinsters in spas do it,
Duchesses when opening bazaars do it,
Let's do it, let's fall in love.

Famous writers in swarms do it,
Somerset and all the Maughams do it,
Let's do it, let's fall in love.
The Brontës felt that they must do it,
Ernest Hemingway could just do it,
Let's do it, let's fall in love.
E. Allan Poe, ho! ho! ho! did it,
But he did it in verse
They say Cocteau did it
But he had to rehearse,
Tennessee Williams self-taught does it,
Kinsey with a deafening report does it,
Let's do it, let's fall in love.

In the Spring of the year
Inhibitions disappear
And our hearts beat high,
We had better face facts
Every gland that overacts
Has an alibi,
For each bird and each bee,
Each slap-happy sappy tree,
Each temptation that lures us along
Is just Nature elle-même
Merely singing us the same
Old song.

In Texas some of the men do it,
Others drill a hole and then do it,
Let's do it, let's fall in love.
They say that each hen and cock does it,
Bernard Miles in Puddle Dock does it,
Let's do it, let's fall in love.
My kith and kin, more or less, do it,
Every uncle and aunt,
But I confess to it,
I've one cousin that can't.
Each tiny clam you consume does it,
Even Liberace we assume does it,
Let's do it, let's fall in love.

The House of Commons en bloc do it,
Civil Servants by the clock do it,
Let's do it, let's fall in love.
Deacons who've done it before do it,
Minor canons with a roar do it,
Let's do it, let's fall in love.
Some rather rorty old rips do it
When they get a bit tight,
Government Whips do it
If it takes them all night,
Harold Wilson out loud does it,
Even Edward Heath on *Morning Cloud* does it,
Let's do it, let's fall in love.
Teenagers squeezed into jeans do it,
Probably we'll live to see machines do it,
Let's do it, let's fall in love.

RON REID

First sung by the Author in cabaret, 1955

53

𝄞 ALICE IS

In a dear little village, remote and obscure
A beautiful maiden resided,
As to whether or not her intentions were pure
Opinion was sharply divided.
She loved to lie out 'neath the darkening sky
And allow the soft breeze to entrance her,
She whispered her dreams to the birds flying by
But seldom received any answer.

Over the field and along the lane
Gentle Alice would love to stray,
When it came to the end of the day,
She would wander away, unheeding,
Dreaming her innocent dreams she strolled,
Quite unaffected by heat or cold,
Frequently freckled or soaked with rain,
Alice was out in the lane.
Whom she met there
Every day there,
Was a question answered by none.
But she'd get there
And she'd stay there
Till whatever she did
Was undoubtedly done.
Over the field and along the lane
When her parents had called in vain,
Sadly, sorrowfully, they'd complain,
'Alice is at it again'.

T IT AGAIN

Though that dear little village
Surrounded by trees
Had neither a school nor a college
Gentle Alice acquired from the birds and the bees
Some exceedingly practical knowledge.
The curious secrets that nature revealed
She refused to allow to upset her
But she thought when observing the beasts of the field
That things might have been organized better.

Over the field and along the lane
Gentle Alice would make up
And take up – her stand.
The road was not exactly arterial
But it led to a town nearby
Where quite a lot of Masculine material
Caught her roving eye.
She was ready to hitchhike,
Cadillac or motor bike.
She wasn't proud or choosy,
All she
Was aiming to be
Was a prinked up
Minked up
Fly-by-night floozie.
When old Rajahs
Gave her pearls as large as
Nuts on a chestnut tree,
All she said was 'Fiddle-dee-dee,
The wages of sin will be the death of me!'
Over the field and along the lane,
Gentle Alice's parents would wait
    hand in hand.
Her dear old white-headed mother,
    wistfully sipping champagne,
Said, 'We've spoiled our child – spared
    the rod,
Open up the caviar and say Thank God,
We've got no cause to complain,
Alice is at it – Alice is at it – Alice is
    at it again.'

Sung by the Author in cabaret, 1955

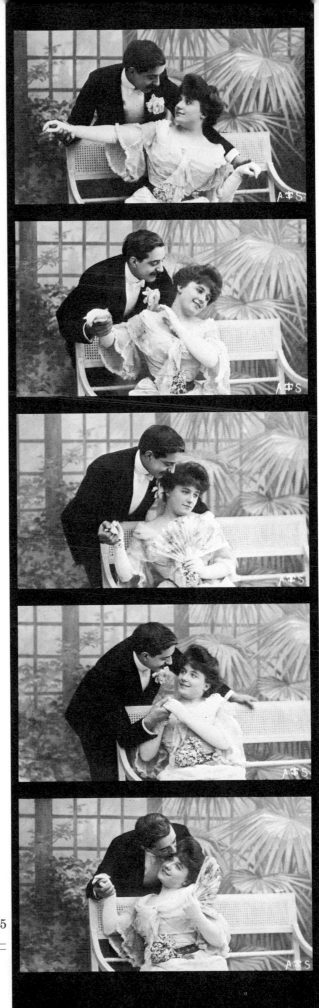

𝄞 MAD ABOUT THE BOY

Society Woman

I met him at a party just a couple of years ago,
He was rather over-hearty and ridiculous
But as I'd seen him on the Screen
He cast a certain spell.
I basked in his attraction for a couple of hours or so,
His manners were a fraction too meticulous,
If he was real or not I couldn't tell
But like a silly fool, I fell.

Mad about the boy,
I know it's stupid to be mad about the boy,
I'm so ashamed of it
But must admit
The sleepless nights I've had about the boy.
On the Silver Screen
He melts my foolish heart in every single scene.
Although I'm quite aware
That here and there
Are traces of the cad about the boy,
Lord knows I'm not a fool girl,
I really shouldn't care,
Lord knows I'm not a schoolgirl
In the flurry of her first affair.
Will it ever cloy?
This odd diversity of misery and joy,
I'm feeling quite insane
And young again
And all because I'm mad about the boy.

Schoolgirl

Mad about the boy,
It's simply scrumptious to be mad
    about the boy,
I know that quite sincerely
Housman really
Wrote *The Shropshire Lad* about the boy.
In my English Prose
I've done a tracing of his forehead
    and his nose
And there is, honour bright,
A certain slight
Effect of Galahad about the boy.
I've talked to Rosie Hooper,
She feels the same as me,
She says that Gary Cooper
Doesn't thrill her to the same degree.
In *Can Love Destroy?*
When he meets Garbo in a suit of corduroy,
He gives a little frown
And knocks her down,
Oh dear, oh dear, I'm mad about the boy.

Cockney

Mad about the boy,
I know I'm potty but I'm mad about the boy.
He sets me 'eart on fire
With love's desire,
In fact I've got it bad about the boy.
When I do the rooms
I see 'is face in all the brushes and
    the brooms.
Last week I strained me back
And got the sack
And 'ad a row with Dad about the boy.
I'm finished with Navarro,
I'm tired of Richard Dix,
I'm pierced by Cupid's arrow
Every Wednesday from four till six.
'Ow I should enjoy
To let 'im treat me like a plaything or a toy,
I'd give my all to him
And crawl to him,
So 'elp me Gawd I'm mad about the boy.

Tart

It seems a little silly
For a girl of my age and weight
To walk down Piccadilly
In a haze of love.
It ought to take a good deal more to get a bad girl down,
I should have been exempt, for
My particular kind of Fate
Has taught me such contempt for
Every phase of love,
And now I've been and spent my last half-crown
To weep about a painted clown.
Mad about the boy,
It's pretty funny but I'm mad about the boy,
He has a gay appeal
That makes me feel
There's maybe something sad about the boy.
Walking down the street,
His eyes look out at me from people that I meet,
I can't believe it's true
But when I'm blue
In some strange way I'm glad about the boy.
I'm hardly sentimental,
Love isn't so sublime,
I have to pay my rental
And I can't afford to waste much time.
If I could employ
A little magic that would finally destroy
This dream that pains me
And enchains me
But I can't because I'm mad about the boy.

Sung by Joyce Barbour, Norah Howard,
Doris Hare and Steffi Duna in
Words and Music, 1932

𝄞 ANY LITTLE FISH

I've fallen in love with you;
I'm taking it badly,
Freezing, burning,
Tossing, turning,
Never know when to laugh or cry,
Just look what our dumb friends do, they welcome it gladly.
Passion in a dromedary doesn't go so deep,
Camels when they're mating never sob themselves to sleep,
Buffaloes can revel in it, so can any sheep;
Why can't I?

Any little fish can swim, any little bird can fly,
Any little dog and any little cat
Can do a bit of this and just a bit of that;
Any little horse can neigh, and any little cow can moo,
But I can't do anything at all,
But just love you.

Any little cock can crow, any little fox can run,
Any little crab on any little shore
Can have a little dab and then a little more;
Any little owl can hoot, and any little dove can coo,
But I can't do anything at all but just love you.

Any little bug can bite, any little bee can buzz,
Any little snail on any little oak,
Can feel a little frail and have a little joke;
Any little frog can jump like any little kangaroo,
But I can't do anything at all but just love you.

Any little duck can quack, any little worm can crawl,
Any little mole can frolic in the sun,
And make a little hole and have a little fun;
Any little snake can hiss in any little local zoo,
But I can't do anything at all but just love you.

Sung by Ada-May in *Charles B. Cochran's 1931 Revue*, 1931

Barnaby I'll have to get the bees and birds to tell you
That I've loved you from the start,
I simply haven't got the words to tell you
What is truly in my heart,
Joking apart.
When you want me – if you want me
Call me – call me – if you care.
When you need me – if you need me
Say so – say so – I'll be there.
I've nothing but my heart to bring to you,
No money but a questing mind,
But if this little song I sing to you
Means a thing to you
Please be kind.
When you're lonely – if you're lonely
Call me – call me – anyhow.
If you want me – need me – love me
Tell me,
Tell me,
Tell me now!

♪ WHEN YOU WANT ME

Nancy I'll love you longer than *The Forsyte Saga*
And I'll tremble at your frown.

Barnaby I'd like to cable to Balenciaga
To prepare your wedding gown,
Don't let me down.

Nancy I want to make my feelings clear to you,
I've never felt like this before.

Barnaby I'd sacrifice my whole career to you
To be near to you
Evermore.

Nancy & Barnaby When you're lonely – if you're lonely
Call me – call me – anyhow.

If you want me – need me – love me
Tell me – tell me – here and now!

Barnaby I really haven't any goods and chattels
But a beat-up Chevrolet.

Nancy I only know I've got a heart that rattles
Every time you look my way.

Nancy & Barnaby There's really nothing more to say
Except that I should like to stay
With you for ever and a day,
Olé!

Sung by Patricia Harty and Grover Dale in *Sail Away*, New York, 1961

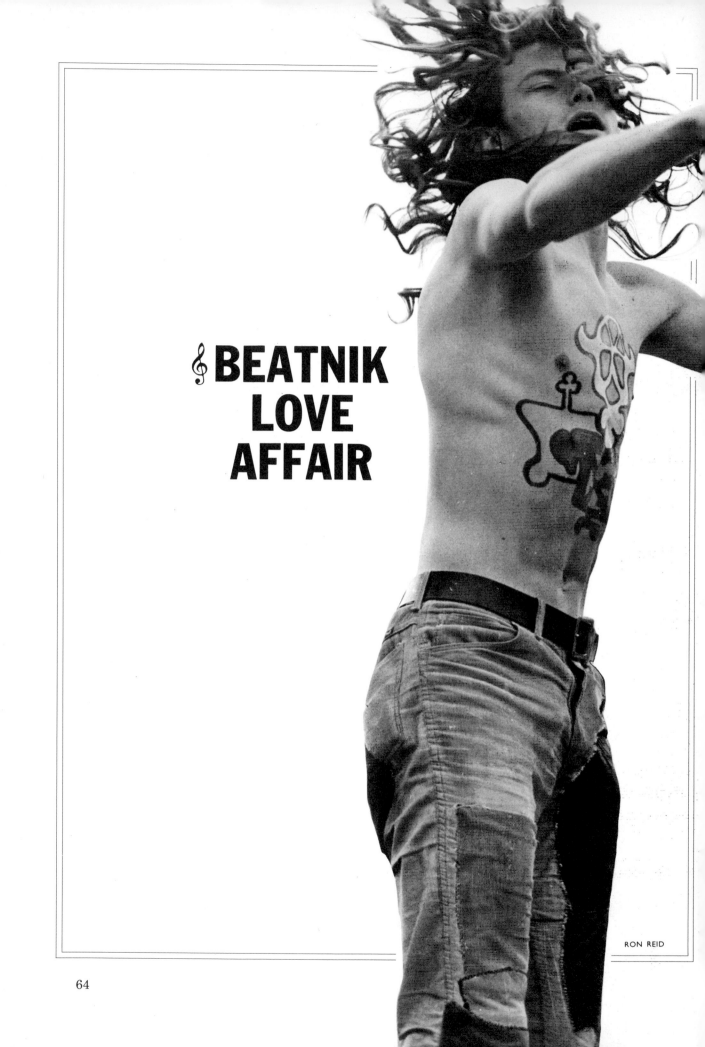

♪BEATNIK LOVE AFFAIR

RON REID

64

Why suffer from moral convictions?
Social restrictions?
Let's thumb our noses at
Cold Wars and atomic predictions.
They're only a waste of time.
Let's make a romantic decision,
Follow a vision,
Now is the moment to see clearly
And realize that really
We are on the brink of it,
Come to think of it.

You and I could have an upright, downright,
Watertight, Dynamite
Love affair.
We could either play it up-beat, down-beat,
On-the-beat, off-the-beat,
Fair or square.
Hey for those flip Calypsos,
Ho for that rhythmic din,
Heigho for those dopes and dipsos,
Rum punch, coconuts, Gordon's gin

Think if we tried out
Some little hide-out
On some tropical isle.
Naked and warm
From dawn to moonrise,
Somerset Maugham-wise,
Blue Lagoon-wise.
We could lie upon the beach at nights, dear,
Watching all those Russian satellites, dear,
Whizzing through the air
While we carried on with our off-beat, on-beat, Beatnik
Love affair.

You and I could have an in-board, out-board,
Overboard, bed-and-board
Love affair,
All we need's a little off-key, on-key,
King-sized, organized
Time to spare,
There by the Caribbean
We'll cross the Rubicon.
We'll have, by the deep blue sea, an
All-out roustabout carry-on.
We'll get a 'Man-Tan',
Gargantuan tan
On those shimmering sands.
Nothing to do but read and rest, dear,
We could get through *By Love Possessed*, dear,
Every time we hear a seagull whistle
We'll forget our last misguided missile
Just destroyed Times Square,
As we carry on with our king-sized, organized,
Beatnik Love Affair . . .

Sung by Grover Dale and Patricia Harty in *Sail Away*, New York, 1961

♪ LOUISA

Louisa was a movie queen.
Before she'd achieved the age of sweet sixteen,
Long before Cagney threw those girls about,
Little Louisa tossed her curls about.
Later when the talkies came
The whole world
Resounded with her fame,
Each time she married
Every daily paper carried
Headlines blazing her name.
Not only headlines
But photographs and interviews,
Everything she did was news
That held the world in thrall.

Some said she read lines
Better than Marlene could,
No other entertainer could
Compare with her at all.
But regardless of the fact
That she could sing and dance and act
And owned furniture that wasn't 'Little Rockery',
And regardless of her gems,
Which were hers, not M.G.M.'s,
Her life was one long mockery.

Louisa was terribly lonely,
Success brought her naught but despair.
She derived little fun from the Oscars she'd won
And none from her home in Bel Air.
She declared she was weary of living
On a bestial terrestrial plane.
When friends came to visit their hands she would clutch
Crying, 'Tell me, why is it I suffer so much?
If only, if only, if only
My life wasn't quite such a strain.'
And soon after that she was terribly lonely,
All over again.

Louisa was terribly lonely,
Louisa was terribly sad.
It appears that the cheers that had rung in her ears
For years had been driving her mad.
She sobbed when men offered her sables
And moaned when they gave her champagne.
She remarked to her groom on their
    honeymoon night
As he tenderly kissed her and turned out the light,
'If only, if only, if only
I'd thrown myself out of the plane . . .'
The very next day she was terribly lonely,
All over again . . .

Sung by the Author in cabaret, 1957

This Blessed Plot

𝄞 THE STATELY HOMES OF ENGLAND

Lord Elderley, Lord Borrowmere,
Lord Sickert and Lord Camp
With every virtue, every grace,
Ah what avails the sceptred race,
Here you see – the four of us,
And there are so many more of us,
Eldest sons that must succeed.
We know how Caesar conquered Gaul
And how to whack a cricket ball;
Apart from this, our education
Lacks co-ordination.
Though we're young and tentative,
And rather rip-representative,
Scions of a noble breed,
We are the products of those homes
    serene and stately,
Which only lately,
Seem to have run to seed!

The stately homes of England,
How beautiful they stand,
To prove the upper classes
Have still the upper hand;

Though the fact that they have to be rebuilt
And frequently mortgaged to the hilt
Is inclined to take the gilt
Off the gingerbread,
And certainly damps the fun
Of the eldest son –
But still we won't be beaten,
We'll scrimp and scrape and save,
The playing-fields of Eton
Have made us frightfully brave –
And though if the Van Dycks have to go
And we pawn the Bechstein grand,
We'll stand
By the stately homes of England.

Here you see
The pick of us,
You may be heartily sick of us.
Still with sense
We're all imbued.
Our homes command extensive views
And with assistance from the Jews
We have been able to dispose of
Rows and rows and rows of
Gainsboroughs and Lawrences,
Some sporting prints of Aunt Florence's,
Some of which were rather rude.
Although we sometimes flaunt our
    family conventions,
Our good intentions
Mustn't be misconstrued.

The stately homes of England
We proudly represent,
We only keep them up for
Americans to rent.
Though the pipes that supply the bathroom burst
And the lavatory makes you fear the worst,
It was used by Charles the First,
Quite informally,
And later by George the Fourth
On a journey North.
The state apartments keep their
Historical renown,
It's wiser not to sleep there
In case they tumble down;
But still if they ever catch on fire

Which, with any luck they might
We'll fight
For the stately homes of England.

The stately homes of England,
Though rather in the lurch,
Provide a lot of chances
For Psychical Research –
There's the ghost of a crazy younger son
Who murdered, in thirteen fifty-one,
An extremely rowdy nun
Who resented it,
And people who come to call
Meet her in the hall.
The baby in the guest wing,
Who crouches by the grate,
Was walled up in the west wing
In fourteen twenty-eight.
If anyone spots
The Queen of Scots

In a hand-embroidered shroud
We're proud
Of the stately homes of England.

Lord Elderley, Lord Borrowmere,
Lord Sickert and Lord Camp,
Behold us in our hours of ease,
Uncertain, coy and hard to please.
Reading in Debrett of us,
This fine patrician quartette of us,
We can feel extremely proud,
Our ancient lineage we trace,
Back to the cradle of the race
Before those beastly Roman bowmen
Bitched our local yeomen.
Though our new democracy
May pain the old Aristocracy
We've not winced nor cried aloud,
Under the bludgeonings of chance
     what will be – will be.
Our heads will still be
Bloody but quite unbowed!

The stately homes of England,
Although a trifle bleak,
Historically speaking,
Are more or less unique.
We've a cousin who won the Golden Fleece
And a very peculiar fowling-piece
Which was sent to Cromwell's niece,
Who detested it,
And rapidly sent it back
With a dirty crack.
A note we have from Chaucer
Contains a bawdy joke.
We also have a saucer
That Bloody Mary broke.
We've two pairs of tights
King Arthur's Knights
Had completely worn away.
Sing Hey!
For the stately homes of England!

Sung by
Hugh French, Ross Landon, John Gatrell
and Kenneth Carten in *Operette*, 1938

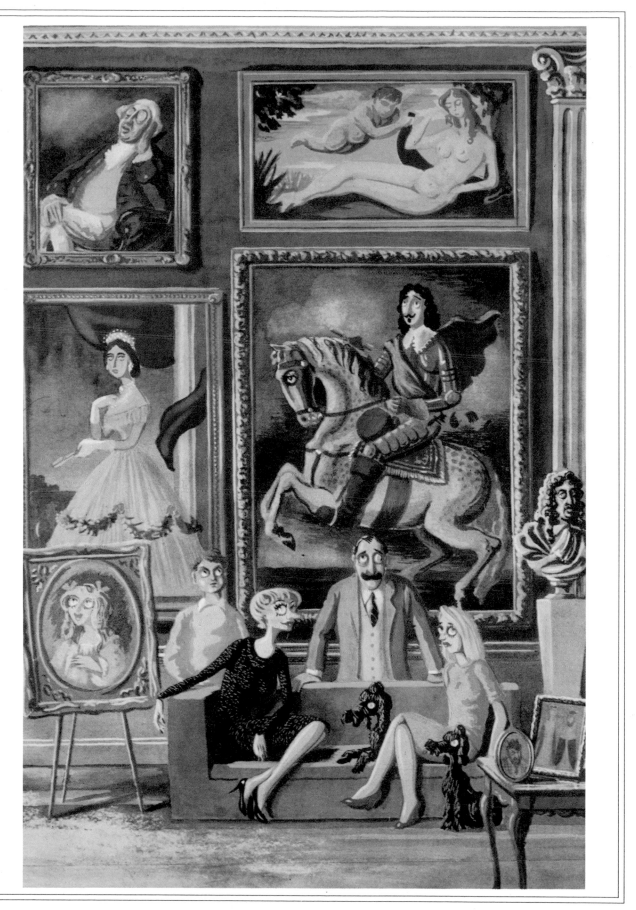

The Littlehamptons at Home, by Osbert Lancaster, 1957

The Local, by Edward Ardizzone, R.A.

♪ SATURDAY NIGHT AT THE ROSE AND CROWN

Saturday night at the Rose and Crown
That's just the place to be,
Tinkers and Tailors
And Soldiers and Sailors
All out for a bit of a spree,
If you find that you're
Weary of life
With your trouble and strife
And the kids have got you down,
It will all come right
On Saturday night
At the Rose and Crown.

Sung by Tessie O'Shea in
The Girl Who Came to Supper, 1962

75

RETURN TO LONDON

London as a city had in the past never attracted me much. It was my home, of course, and I knew it intimately, perhaps too intimately. In my early days I had known its seamy side and later on more of its graces, but it had always seemed to me a little dull and smug compared with the romantic gaiety of Paris and the sharp vitality of New York. Now suddenly, in my early forties, I saw it for the first time as somewhere I belonged. This sentimental revelation was made clearer to me by the fact that I was staying in a London hotel for the first time in my life. It was a strange sensation to step out of the comfortable impersonality of the Savoy into the personal familiar streets of my childhood. I felt a sudden urge to visit the Tower and the Abbey and Madame Tussaud's and to go to the zoo. The move from Gerald Road to the Strand had transformed me overnight into a tourist in my own home, and as such it seemed more attractive to me and more genuinely gay than it had ever been before. I am not sure that that particular quality of gaiety survived the war. The rigours of peace and post-war party politics have done much to dim its glow, but in 1941 the real lights of London shone through the blackout with a steady brilliance that I shall never forget.

Future Indefinite, 1954

London – is a little bit of all right,
Nobody can deny that's true,
Bow Bells – Big Ben,
Up to the heath and down again,
And if you should visit the monkeys in the zoo
Bring a banana.
Feed the ducks in Battersea Park
Or take a trip to Kew,
It only costs a tanner there and back,
Watch our lads in the Palace Yard
Troop the Colour and Change the Guard
And don't forget your brolly and your mack:
And I'd like to mention
London – is a place where you can call right
Round and have a cosy cup of tea,
And if you're fed right up and got your tail right down,
London Town
Is a wonderful place to be.

♪ LONDON IS A LITTLE BIT OF ALL RIGHT

MAX GREEN

London – is a little bit of all right,
Nobody can deny that's so,
Big Ben – Bow Bells,
Have a good laugh and watch the swells
Treating themselves to a trot in Rotten Row
Sitting on horses.
Grosvenor Square or Petticoat Lane,
Belgravia, Peckham Rye,
You can stray through any neighbourhood,
If you haven't a swanky club
Just pop into the nearest pub,
A little of what you fancy does you good,
And I'd like to mention
London – is a place where you can call right
Round and have a cosy cup of tea,
If you use your loaf a bit and know what's what
This old spot
Is a bloody good place to be.

Sung by Tessie O'Shea in
The Girl Who Came to Supper, 1962

MAX GREEN

THE
ROAD
STARS

FIRST CLASS
AWARD

𝄞 LONDON AT NIGHT

London at night
With the gas lamps alight
Is a wonderful sight
For the eye to see
With its clubs and pubs and bars
And the sleepy Thames reflecting the stars,
London at night
Whether sober or tight
Is a sight
That Americans die to see,
From the naphtha flares that glow
In the markets of Soho
To the far less exotic
And more patriotic
Restraint of Pimlico,
London's a place
That your heart can embrace
If your heart is free
And prone to be
Receptive to delight,
Rome was once gay
In a decadent way
But we're sure that it never was quite
Like London at night.

Sung by Donald Scott, Dennis Bower, Tom Gill, Graham Payn,
Peter Graves and Shamus Locke in *After the Ball*, 1954

𝄞 WHAT HO, MRS BRISKET

What ho, Mrs Brisket,
Why not take a plunge and risk it?
The water's warm
There ain't no crabs
And you'll have a lot of fun among the shrimps and dabs.
If for a lark
Some saucy old shark
Takes a nibble at your chocolate biscuit
Swim for the shore
And the crowd will roar
What ho, Mrs Brisket!

Sung by Tessie O'Shea in
The Girl Who Came to Supper, 1962

Could you please oblige us with a Bren gun?
The lack of one is wounding to our pride.
Last night we found the cutest
Little German parachutist
Who looked at our kit
And giggled a bit
Then laughed until he cried . . .
On Sunday's mock invasion Captain Clarke was heard to say
He hadn't even got a brush and comb;
So if you can't oblige us with a Bren gun –
The Home Guard might as well go home.

Sung by the Author, 1941

♪ COULD YOU PLEASE OBLIGE US WITH A BREN GUN?

♪ DON'T TAKE OUR CHARLIE FOR THE ARMY

Don't take our Charlie for the Army,
He's a sensitive lad,
And like his Dad
His heart is far from strong,
He couldn't do route marches,
On account of his fallen arches
And his asthma's something terrible
When the winter comes along.
He's a nice boy – one of the best,
But when he gets a cold on his chest
He coughs until he nearly drives us barmy,
So nightie-night – close the door,
Go back to the barracks and think some more
Before you take our Charlie for the Army.

Sung by Tessie O'Shea in *The Girl Who Came to Supper*, 1962

THERE ARE BAD TIMES JUST AROUND THE CORNER

They're out of sorts in Sunderland
And terribly cross in Kent,
They're dull in Hull
And the Isle of Mull
Is seething with discontent,
They're nervous in Northumberland
And Devon is down the drain,
They're filled with wrath
On the Firth of Forth
And sullen on Salisbury Plain,
In Dublin they're depressed, lads,
Maybe because they're Celts
For Drake is going West, lads,
And so is everyone else.
Hurray – hurray – hurray!
Misery's here to stay.

There are bad times just around the corner,
There are dark clouds hurtling through the sky
And it's no good whining
About a silver lining
For we know from experience that they won't roll by.
With a scowl and a frown
We'll keep our peckers down
And prepare for depression and doom and dread,
We're going to unpack our troubles from our old kit bag
And wait until we drop down dead.

From Portland Bill to Scarborough
They're querulous and subdued
And Shropshire lads
Have behaved like cads
From Berwick-on-Tweed to Bude,
They're mad at Market Harborough
And livid at Leigh-on-Sea,
In Tunbridge Wells
You can hear the yells
Of woe-begone bourgeoisie.
We all get bitched about, lads,
Whoever our vote elects,
We know we're up the spout, lads,
And that's what England expects.
Hurray – hurray – hurray!
Trouble is on the way.

There are bad times just around the corner,
The horizon's gloomy as can be,
There are black birds over
The greyish cliffs of Dover
And the rats are preparing to leave the B.B.C.
We're an *un*happy breed
And very bored indeed
When reminded of something that Nelson said.
While the press and the politicians nag nag nag
We'll wait until we drop down dead.

'You've never had it so good'

From Colwyn Bay to Kettering
They're sobbing themselves to sleep,
The shrieks and wails
In the Yorkshire dales
Have even depressed the sheep.
In rather vulgar lettering
A very disgruntled group
Have posted bills
On the Cotswold Hills
To prove that we're in the soup.
While begging Kipling's pardon
There's one thing we know for sure
If England is a garden
We ought to have more manure.
Hurray – hurray – hurray!
Suffering and dismay.

There are bad times just around the corner
And the outlook's absolutely vile,
There are Home Fires smoking
From Windermere to Woking
And we're *not* going to tighten our belts and smile smile smile,
At the sound of a shot
We'd just as soon as not
Take a hot water bottle and go to bed,
We're going to *un*tense our muscles till they sag sag sag
And wait until we drop down dead.

There are bad times just around the corner,
We can all look forward to despair,
It's as clear as crystal
From Bridlington to Bristol
That we can't save democracy and we don't much care
If the Reds and the Pinks
Believe that England stinks
And that world revolution is bound to spread,
We'd better all learn the lyrics of the old 'Red Flag'
And wait until we drop down dead.
A likely story
Land of Hope and Glory,
Wait until we drop down dead.

Sung by Graham Payn, Dora Bryan, Joan Heal and
Ian Carmichael in *The Globe Revue*, 1952

The burning of St Clement Dane's, 1941, by Henry Carr

♪ LONDON PRIDE

London Pride has been handed down to us.
London Pride is a flower that's free.
London Pride means our own dear town to us,
And our pride it for ever will be.
Grey city,
Stubbornly implanted,
Taken so for granted
For a thousand years.
Stay, city,
Smokily enchanted,
Cradle of our memories and hopes and fears.
Every Blitz
Your resistance
Toughening,
From the Ritz
To the Anchor and Crown,
Nothing ever could override
The pride of London Town.

Sung by Binnie Hale in
Up and Doing, 1941

A.R.P. Warden, 1941, by Feliks Topolski

Travel poster, 1927, by A. M. Cassandre

S.O.S. Drawing by Jean Cocteau

I love travelling, but I'm always too late or too early. I arrive in Japan when the cherry blossoms have fallen. I get to China too early for the next revolution. I reach Canada when the maple leaves have gone. People are always telling me about something I haven't seen. I find it very pleasant.

1st American Lady Oh, my Verner's sharp enough in business, I'll grant you that, but he just won't open his arms out to *experience*. I mean he deliberately shuts his eyes to the *beauty* of things. You'd never credit it, but in the whole five months we've been in Europe this trip, he's only been inside three churches.

2nd American Lady Perhaps he doesn't like churches.

1st American Lady I managed to drag him into Saint Peter's in Rome and all he did was stomp around humming 'I like New York in June' under his breath. I was mortified.

Come into the Garden, Maud, in *Suite in Three Keys*, 1965

She My father was stationed in Darjeeling when I was born.

He Nice place, Darjeeling.

She Do you know it?

He No. But a friend of mine shot himself through the foot there once.
He spoke very highly of it.

South Sea Bubble, 1956

USELESS USEFUL PHRASES

Pray tell me the time,
It is six,
It is seven,
It's half past eleven,
It's twenty to two,
I want thirteen stamps
Does your child have convulsions?
Please bring me some rhubarb
I need a shampoo.
How much is that hat?
I desire some red stockings,
My mother is married,
These boots are too small,
My Aunt has a cold,
Shall we go to the Opera?
This meat is disgusting,
Is this the Town Hall?

My cousin is deaf,
Kindly bring me a hatchet,
Pray pass me the pepper,
What pretty cretonne,
What time is the train?
It is late,
It is early,
It's running on schedule,
It's here,
It has gone . . .

This mutton is tough,
There's a mouse in my bedroom,
This egg is delicious,
This soup is too thick,
Please bring me a trout,
What an excellent pudding,
Pray hand me my gloves,
I'm going to be sick!

Sung by Elaine Stritch in *Sail Away*, 1961–6

♪ WHY DO THE WRONG PEOPLE TRAVEL?

MAX GREEN

Travel they say improves the mind,
An irritating platitude
Which frankly, entre nous,
Is very far from true.
Personally I've yet to find
That longitude and latitude
Can educate those scores
Of monumental bores
Who travel in groups and herds and troupes
Of various breeds and sexes,
Till the whole world reels
To shouts and squeals
And the clicking of Rolliflexes.

Why do the wrong people travel, travel, travel,
When the right people stay back home?
What compulsion compels them
And who the hell tells them
To drag their cans to Zanzibar
Instead of staying quietly in Omaha?
The Taj Mahal
And the Grand Canal
And the sunny French Riviera
Would be less oppressed
If the Middle West
Would settle for somewhere rather nearer.
Please do not think that I criticize or cavil
At a genuine urge to roam,
But why oh why do the wrong people travel
When the right people stay back home
And mind their business,
When the right people stay back home
With Cinerama,
When the right people stay back home,
I'm merely asking
Why the right people stay back home?

95

Just when you think romance is ripe
It rather sharply dawns on you
That each sweet serenade
Is for the Tourist Trade.
Any attractive native type
Who resolutely fawns on you
Will give as his address
American Express.
There isn't a rock
Between Bangkok
And the beaches of Hispaniola,
That does not recoil
From suntan oil
And the gurgle of Coca Cola.

Why do the wrong people travel, travel, travel,
When the right people stay back home?
What explains this mass mania
To leave Pennsylvania
And clack around like flocks of geese,
Demanding dry martinis on the Isles of Greece?
In the smallest street
Where the gourmets meet
They invariably fetch up
And it's hard to make
Them accept a steak
That isn't served rare and smeared with ketchup.
Millions of tourists are churning up the gravel
While they gaze at St Peter's dome,
But why oh why do the wrong people travel
When the right people stay back home
And eat hot doughnuts,
When the right people stay back home
With all those benefits,
When the right people stay back home?
I sometimes wonder
Why the right people stay back home!

Why do the wrong people travel, travel, travel,
When the right people stay back home?
What peculiar obsessions
Inspire those processions
Of families from Houston, Tex,
With all those cameras around their necks?
They will take a train
Or an aeroplane
For an hour on the Costa Brava,
And they'll see Pompeii
On the only day
That it's up to its ass in molten lava.
It would take years to unravel – ravel – ravel
Every impulse that makes them roam
But why oh why do the wrong people travel
When the right people stay back home
With all that Kleenex,
When the right people stay back home
With all that lettuce,
When the right people stay back home
With all those Kennedys?
Won't someone tell me
Why the right,
I say the right people stay back home?

Sung by Elaine Stritch in *Sail Away*, 1961–62

THE PASSENGER'S ALWAYS RIGHT

Joe

In the course of each cruise
I always choose
To lecture each subordinate.
You're not damned fools
And you know the rules,
So see you all co-ordinate.

Stewards

We've heard all this before.

Hoskins

I can't stand any more.

Joe

Bow, smile, charm, tact,
Never forget one vital fact:

The passenger's always right, my boys,
The passenger's always right.
Although he's a drip
He's paid for his trip
So greet him with delight.
Agree to his suggestions,
However coarse or crude.
Reply to all his questions,
Ply him with drink – stuff him with food.
The passenger may be sober, boys,
The passenger may be tight,
The passenger may be foe or friend
Or absolutely round the bend,
But calm him,
Charm him,
Even though he's higher than a kite,
The passenger's always right.

Carrington

The woman in cabin forty-nine has lost
    her diamond brooch.

Joe

Calm her, Carrington,
Charm her, Carrington,
That's the correct approach.

Hoskins

A gentleman on the Promenade Deck
    just called me a lazy slob.

Joe

Smile at him, Hoskins,
Smile at him, Hoskins,
That is part of your job.

Steward

The three fat children in B Deck 3
Have thrown their bathmat in the sea.

Shuttleworth

The silly old broad in Main Deck 2
Has dropped her dentures down the loo.

Joe

Passengers since the world began
Have been querulous, rude and snooty.
England expects that every man
This day should do his duty . . .

The passenger's always right, my boys,
The passenger's always right.
Those dreary old wrecks
Who litter the decks
Demand that you're polite.
Don't count on any free time
Be kind to all the jerks,
And every day at teatime,
Stuff 'em with cake . . . give 'em the works.

The passenger may be dull, my boys,
The passenger may be bright,
The passenger may be quite serene
Or gibbering with Benzedrine,
But nurse him,
Curse him
Only when the bastard's out of sight,
Remember boys,
The goddamned passenger's always right.

Sung by Charles Braswell and the stewards in
          Sail Away, New York, 1961

In tropical climes there are certain times of day
When all the citizens retire
To tear their clothes off and perspire,
It's one of those rules that the greatest fools obey,
Because the sun is much too sultry
And one must avoid its ultry-violet ray.

Papalaka papalaka papalaka boo,
Papalaka papalaka papalaka boo,
Digariga digariga digariga doo,
Digariga, digariga, digariga doo!

The natives grieve when the white men leave their huts,
Because they're obviously, definitely nuts!

Mad dogs and Englishmen
Go out in the midday sun,
The Japanese don't care to,
The Chinese wouldn't dare to,
Hindoos and Argentines sleep firmly from twelve to one,
But Englishmen detest a siesta.
In the Philippines
There are lovely screens
To protect you from the glare,
In the Malay States
There are hats like plates
Which the Britishers won't wear.
At twelve noon
The natives swoon
And no further work is done,
But mad dogs and Englishmen
Go out in the midday sun.

It's such a surprise for the Eastern eyes to see
That though the English are effete
They're quite impervious to heat,
When the white man rides every native hides in glee,
Because the simple creatures hope he
Will impale his solar topee on a tree.

Bolyboly bolyboly bolyboly baa,
Bolyboly, bolyboly, bolyboly baa,
Habaninny, habaninny, habaninny haa,
Habaninny, habaninny, habaninny haa.

𝄞 **MAD DOGS AND ENGLISHMEN**

It seems such a shame
When the English claim
The earth
That they give rise to such hilarity
    and mirth.

Mad dogs and Englishmen
Go out in the midday sun.
The toughest Burmese bandit
Can never understand it.
In Rangoon the heat of noon
Is just what the natives shun,
They put their Scotch or Rye down
And lie down.

In a jungle town
Where the sun beats down
To the rage of man and beast
The English garb
Of the English sahib
Merely gets a bit more creased.
In Bangkok
At twelve o'clock
They foam at the mouth and run,
But mad dogs and Englishmen
Go out in the midday sun.

Mad dogs and Englishmen
Go out in the midday sun.
The smallest Malay rabbit
Deplores this stupid habit.
In Hongkong
They strike a gong
And fire off a noonday gun
To reprimand each inmate
Who's in late.

In the mangrove swamps
Where the python romps
There is peace from twelve to two,
Even caribous
Lie around and snooze
For there's nothing else to do.
In Bengal
To move at all
Is seldom, if ever done,
But mad dogs and Englishmen
Go out in the midday sun.

Sung by Beatrice Lillie in
New York in *The Third
Little Show*, 1931, and by
Romney Brent in London
in *Words and Music,* 1932

𝄞 I WONDER WHAT HAPPENED TO HIM

The India that one read about
And may have been misled about
In one respect has kept itself intact.
Though 'Pukka Sahib' traditions may have cracked
And thinned
The good old Indian army's still a fact.
That famous monumental man
The Officer and Gentleman
Still lives and breathes and functions from Bombay to
    Katmandu.
At any moment one can glimpse
Matured or embryonic 'Blimps'
Vivaciously speculating as to what became of who.
Though Eastern sounds may fascinate your ear
When West meets West you're always sure to hear –

Whatever became of old Bagot?
I haven't seen him for a year.
Is it true that young Forbes had to marry that Faggot
He met in the Vale of Kashmir?
Have you had any news
Of that chap in the 'Blues',
Was it Prosser or Pyecroft or Pym?
He was stationed in Simla, or was it Bengal?
I know he got tight at a ball in Nepal
And wrote several four-letter words on the wall.
I wonder what happened to him!

Whatever became of old Shelley?
Is it true that young Briggs was cashiered
For riding quite nude on a push-bike through Delhi
The day the new Viceroy appeared?
Have you had any word
Of that bloke in the 'Third',
Was it Southerby, Sedgwick or Sim?
They had him thrown out of the club in Bombay
For, apart from his mess bills exceeding his pay,
He took to pig-sticking in *quite* the wrong way.
I wonder what happened to him!

One must admit that by and large
Upholders of the British Raj
Don't shine in conversation as a breed.
Though Indian army officers can read
A bit
Their verbal wit – has rather run to seed.
Their splendid insularity
And roguish jocularity
Was echoing through when Victoria
    was Queen.
In restaurants and dining-cars,
In messes, clubs and hotel bars
They try to maintain tradition
    in the way it's always been.
Though worlds may change
    and nations disappear
Above the shrieking chaos
    you will hear –

Whatever became of old Tucker?
Have you heard any word of young Mills
Who ruptured himself at the end of a chukka
And had to be sent to the hills?
They say that young Lees
Had a go of 'D.T.s'
And his hopes of promotion are slim.
According to Stubbs, who's a bit of a louse,
The silly young blighter went out on a 'souse',
And took two old tarts into Government House.
I wonder what happened to him!

Whatever became of old Keeling?
I hear that he got back from France
And frightened three nuns in a train in Darjeeling
By stripping and waving his lance!
D'you remember Munroe,
In the P.A.V.O.?
He was tallish and mentally dim.
That talk of heredity can't be quite true,
He was dropped on his head by his ayah at two,
I presume that by now he'll have reached G.H.Q.
I'm sure that's what happened to him!

Whatever became of old Archie?
I hear he departed this life
After rounding up ten sacred cows
    in Karachi
To welcome the Governor's wife.
D'you remember young Phipps
Who had *very* large hips
And whose waist was excessively slim?
Well, it seems that some doctor
    in Grosvenor Square
Gave him hormone injections
    for growing his hair
And he grew something here, and
    he grew something there.
I wonder what happened to her – him?

Sung by Cyril Ritchard in
Sigh No More, 1945

HENRI CARTIER-BRESSON

I LIKE AMERICA

I like America
I have played around
Every slappy-happy
    hunting-ground,
But I find America – okay . . .
I've roamed the Spanish Main,
Eaten sugar cane,
But I never tasted cellophane
Till I struck the U.S.A.
All delegates
From Southern States
Are nervy and distraught.
In New Orleans
The wrought-iron screens
Are dreadfully overwrought.
Beneath each tree
In Tennessee
Erotic books are read,
And when alligators thud
Through the Mississippi mud
Sex rears its ugly head.
But – I like America,
Every scrap of it,
All the sentimental crap of it,
And come what may,
I shall return one day
To the good old U.S.A.

Sung by Graham Payn in
Ace of Clubs, 1949

Street Crossing – New York, 1928, by John Marin
(*Phillips Gallery, Washington*)

American Gothic, 1930, by Grant Wood
(The Art Institute of Chicago)

BRONXVILLE DARBY AND JOAN

We do not fear the verdict of posterity,
Our lives have been too humdrum and mundane,
In the twilight of our days
Having reached the final phase
In all sincerity
We must explain:

We're a dear old couple and we HATE one another
And we've hated one another for a long, long time.
Since the day that we were wed, up to the present,
Our lives, we must confess,
Have been progressively more unpleasant.

We're just sweet old darlings who despise one another
With a thoroughness approaching the sublime,
But through all our years
We've been affectionately known
As the Bronxville Darby and Joan . . .

We're a dear old couple and we LOATHE one another
With a loathing that engulfs us like a tidal wave,
With our deep sub-conscious minds we seldom dabble
But something *must* impel
The words we spell
When we're playing 'Scrabble'.
We're just sweet old darlings who abhor one another
And we'll bore each other firmly to the grave,
But through all our years we've been affectionately known
As the Bronxville Darby and Joan.

Sung by Sydney Arnold and Edith Day in *Sail Away*, London, 1961

THE NEW WORLD

Come to my country one day . . . It is a great territory, still untamed and rich with promise . . . Oh Lord, the whole of life seems newly washed seen from the open door of a caboose . . . The tail end of a freight train, the last car of all, that is the home of the brakeman. There he sits, watching the trees marching along and the cinders and sand of America slipping away beneath the wheels. He can watch the sun set over the gentle farmlands of Wisconsin and rise over the interminable prairies of Nebraska and Illinois and Kansas. Those flat, flat lands bring the sky so low that on clear nights you can almost feel that you are rattling along through the stars. It is rougher going in the mountains where there are sharp curves and steep gradients and the locomotive strains and gasps and fills the air with steam and sparks; tunnels close around you, infernos of noise and sulphurous smoke, then suddenly you are in the open and can breathe again and there are snow-covered peaks towering above you and pine forests and the sound of waterfalls. Over it all and through it all, the familiar reassuring noise of the train . . . The railroad is my dream, the whole meaning of my life, my pride and all my hopes for the future – come to my country one day. Let me take you in a private car from Chicago to the West . . . and outside the wide windows of your drawing room you shall see the New World passing by . . .

Spoken by Alfred Lunt in *Quadrille*, 1952

𝄞 NINA

Senorita Nina
From Argentina
Knew all the answers,
Although her relatives and friends
    were perfect dancers
She swore she'd never dance a step
    until she died.
She said 'I've seen too many movies
And all they prove is
Too idiotic.
They all insist that South America's exotic,
Whereas it couldn't be more boring if it tried.'
She added firmly that she hated
The sound of soft guitars beside a still lagoon.
She also positively stated
That she could not abide a Southern Moon.
She said with most refreshing candour
That she thought Carmen Miranda
Was subversive propaganda
And should rapidly be shot.

She said she didn't give a jot
If people quoted her or not!
She refused to begin the Beguine when
They requested it,
And she made an embarrassing scene
If anyone suggested it,
For she detested it.
Though no one ever could be keener
Than little Nina
On quite a number
Of very eligible men who did the Rhumba,
When they proposed to her she simply
    left them flat.
She said that love should be impulsive
But not convulsive,
And syncopation
Had a discouraging effect on procreation,
And that she'd rather read a book –
    and that was that!

Senorita Nina
From Argentina
Despised the Tango
And though she never was a girl to let a man go,
She wouldn't sacrifice her principles for sex.
She looked with scorn on the gyrations
Of her relations
Who danced the Conga
And said that if she had to stand it any longer,
She'd lose all dignity and wring their silly necks.
She said that frankly she was blinded
To all their over-advertised romantic charms,
And then she got more bloody-minded
And told them where to put their tropic palms.
She said 'I hate to be pedantic
But it drives me nearly frantic
When I see that unromantic
Sycophantic
Lots of sluts
Forever wriggling their guts
It drives me absolutely nuts!'
She declined to begin the Beguine
Though they besought her to,
And in language profane and obscene

She cursed the man who taught her to;
She cursed Cole Porter too!
From this it's fairly clear that Nina
In her demeanour
Was so offensive
That when the hatred of her friends
  grew too intensive
She thought she'd better beat it while
  she had the chance.
After some trial and tribulation
She reached the station
And met a sailor
Who had acquired a wooden leg
  in Venezuela,
And so she married him because
  he *couldn't* dance!

There surely never could have been a
More irritating girl than Nina,
They never speak in Argentina
Of this degenerate bambina
Who had the luck to find romance
But resolutely wouldn't dance.
She wouldn't dance! – *Hola!*

Sung by Cyril Ritchard in *Sigh No More*, 1945

Party Pieces

B   An excellent dinner darling, I congratulate you.

C   The mousse wasn't quite right.

B   It looked a bit hysterical, but it tasted delicious.

A   Good evening. I missed you at the races on Thursday. What happened to you?

D   I had to attend a family funeral.

A   Oh, how sad for you. I'm so sorry.

D   Please do not be sorry. It was splendid fun. There was a dance afterwards.

A   Not a very close relative, I gather?

D   No. Only a first cousin once and for all removed.

C Have a good flight?

F From the aeronautical point of view, yes. Socially, it left a good deal to be desired.

A Don't you like her?

C No, dear. I detest her. She's far too old for you, and she goes about using sex as a sort of shrimping net.

F What a pretty dress.

G You must have seen it before.

F Of course I have dear, several times; but I'm very fond of it.

A I despise moral attitudes. I believe that life is for living.

B It's difficult to know what else one could do with it.

A Where did you learn to speak such good English?

B The Esplanade Hotel, Bournemouth.

F (*overheard snippet to male guest*) It does seem odd, that with so many attractive women in the world, you should choose one with a bristling cavalry moustache.

G I had an M.G. just after the war, but I ran it into a lorry.

F Butter fingers.

D Really, May, you *must* have heard of Buck Randy.

E He's the rage of America.

C What does he do?

E He sings stripped to the waist with a zither.

B Why should he be stripped to the waist?

D Because he's supposed to have the most beautiful male body in the world, dear.

G Why a zither?

D He accompanies himself on it. Last year one of his records sold two million.

E He has to have police protection everywhere he goes.

A I'm not surprised.

A miscellany of lines from various plays

♪ I'VE BEEN TO A MARVELLOUS PARTY

Quite for no reason
I'm here for the season
And high as a kite,
Living in error
With Maud at Cap Ferrat
Which couldn't be right.
Everyone's here and frightfully gay,
Nobody cares what people say,
Though the Riviera
Seems really much queerer
Than Rome at its height,
Yesterday night –

I've been to a marvellous party
With Nounou and Nada and Nell,
It was in the fresh air
And we went as we were
And we stayed as we were,
Which was Hell.
Poor Grace started singing at midnight
And didn't stop singing till four;
We knew the excitement was bound to begin
When Laura got blind on Dubonnet and gin
And scratched her veneer with a Cartier pin,
I couldn't have liked it more.

I've been to a marvellous party,
I must say the fun was intense,
We all had to do
What the people we knew
Would be doing a hundred years hence.
Dear Cecil arrived wearing armour,
Some shells and a black feather boa,
Poor Millicent wore a surrealist comb
Made of bits of mosaic from St Peter's in Rome,
But the weight was so great that she had to go home,
I couldn't have liked it more!

                    People's behaviour
                    Away from Belgravia
                    Would make you aghast.
                    So much variety
                    Watching Society
                    Scampering past.
                    If you have any mind at all
                    Gibbon's divine *Decline and Fall*
                    Seems pretty flimsy,
                    No more than a whimsy,
                    By way of contrast
                    On Saturday last –

I've been to a marvellous party
We didn't start dinner till ten,
And young Bobbie Carr
Did a stunt at the bar
With a lot of extraordinary men.

Dear Baba arrived with a turtle
Which shattered us all to the core,
The Grand Duke was dancing a foxtrot with me
When suddenly Cyril screamed 'Fiddledidee,'
And ripped off his trousers and jumped into the sea,
I couldn't have liked it more.

> I've been to a marvellous party,
> Elise made an entrance with May,
> You'd never have guessed
> From her fisherman's vest
> That her bust had been whittled away.
> Poor Lulu got fried on Chianti,
> And talked about esprit de corps.
> Maurice made a couple of passes at Gus
> And Freddie, who hates any kind of a fuss,
> Did half the Big Apple and twisted his truss,
> I couldn't have liked it more!

I've been to a marvellous party,
We played the most wonderful game,
Maureen disappeared,
And came back in a beard,
And we all had to guess at her name!
We talked about growing old gracefully,
And Elsie, who's seventy-four,
Said 'A, it's a question of being sincere,
and B, if you're supple you've nothing to fear,'
Then she swung upside down from a glass chandelier,
I couldn't have liked it more!

Sung by Beatrice Lillie in *Set to Music* and *All Clear*, 1939

SHADOW PLAY

The lights come up on a moonlit garden. There is a stone bench; Vicky and a Young Man are sitting on it.

Vicky	It's nice and cool in the garden.
Young Man	It's nice and cool in the garden.
Vicky	Country-house dances can be lovely when the weather's good, can't they?
Young Man	Rather – rather – yes, of course – rather.
Vicky	I'm waiting for something.
Young Man	Country-house dances can be lovely when the weather's good, can't they?
Vicky	This is where it all began.
Young Man	It's nice and cool in the garden.
Vicky (to herself)	Please hurry, my darling. I can't wait to see you for the first time.
Young Man	Do you know this part of the country?
Vicky	Intimately. I'm staying here with my aunt, you know.
Young Man	Does she ride to hounds?
Vicky	Incessantly.
Young Man	That's ripping, isn't it? I mean, it really is ripping.
Vicky	Yes. She's a big woman and she kills little foxes. She's kind *au fond*, but she dearly loves killing little foxes.
Young Man	We're getting on awfully well – it's awfully nice out here – I think you're awfully pretty.
Vicky (to herself)	This is a waste of time – he should be here by now – walking through the trees – coming towards me.
Young Man	I think you're an absolute fizzer.
Vicky	Yes, I remember you saying that – it made me want to giggle – but I controlled myself beautifully.
Young Man	I think you know my sister – she's in pink.
Vicky	I remember her clearly – a beastly girl . . .
Young Man	I'm so glad you like her – you must come and stay with us – my mother's an absolute fizzer – you'd love her.
Vicky	God forbid!
Young Man	That's absolutely ripping of you.
Vicky (to herself)	Now – now – at last – you're walking through the trees – hurry! *(Simon comes through the trees. He is smoking a cigarette)*
Vicky	I thought you'd missed your entrance.
Simon	Are you engaged for this dance?
Vicky	I was, but I'll cut it if you'll promise to love me always, and never let anything or anybody spoil it – never.
Simon	But of course – that's understood.
Young Man	Will you excuse me? I have to dance with Lady Dukes.
Vicky	Certainly.
Young Man	Good hunting.

Vicky	Thank you so much – it's been so boring.
Young Man	Not at all – later perhaps.

(He goes)

Simon	Well – here we are.
Vicky	The first time – we knew at once – didn't we? Don't you remember how we discussed it afterwards?
Simon	I saw you in the ballroom – I wondered who you were.
Vicky	My name's Victoria – Victoria Marden.
Simon	Mine's Simon Gayforth.
Vicky	How do you do?
Simon	Quite well, thank you.
Vicky	I suppose you came down from London for the dance?
Simon	Yes, I'm staying with the Bursbys.
Vicky	What do you do?
Simon	I'm in a bank.
Vicky	High up in the bank? Or just sitting in a little cage totting up things?
Simon	Oh, quite high up really. It's a very good bank.
Vicky	I'm so glad.
Simon	How lovely you are.
Vicky	No, no, that came later – you've skipped some.
Simon	Sorry.
Vicky	You're nice and thin – your eyes are funny – you move easily. I'm afraid you're terribly attractive.
Simon	You never said that.
Vicky	No, but I thought it.
Simon	Stick to the script.
Vicky	Small talk – a lot of small talk – with quite different thoughts going on behind – this garden's really beautiful – are you good at gardens?
Simon	No, but I'm persevering – I'm all right on the more straightforward blooms – you know, snapdragons, sweet william, cornflowers and tobacco plant – and I can tell a Dorothy Perkins a mile off.
Vicky	That hedge over there is called Cupressus macrocarpa.
Simon	Do you swear it?
Vicky	It grows terribly quickly, but they say that it goes a bit thin underneath in about twenty years.
Simon	How beastly of them to say that – it's slander.
Vicky	Did you know about Valerian smelling of cats?
Simon	You're showing off again.
Vicky	It's true.
Simon	I can go one better than that – Lotuses smell of pineapple.
Vicky	(*sadly*) Everything smells of something else – it's dreadfully confusing.

(Music starts)

Simon	Never mind, darling – I love you desperately – I knew it the first second I saw you –
Vicky	You're skipping again.

Tonight at 8.30: Shadow Play, 1935

Noël Coward and Gertrude Lawrence in *Shadow Play*

LAST WORDS

She I expect you see life quite differently from ordinary people – I mean, being a world-famous writer and having people making a fuss of you all the time.

He They occasionally let up.

She I'm afraid you must have found this evening very dull.

He Not at all. I've enjoyed it immensely.

She You know, I have a dreadful confession to make.

He Confession?

She You'll probably think me absolutely awful, but I just can't bear false pretences and playing up to people; it's just not in my nature.

He Very commendable.

She And anyhow, you're so brilliant and successful, that what I say couldn't matter to you one way or the other, could it?

He That depends what it is.

She Well, it's this – I've read all your books, and, frankly, I didn't care for them.

He Did you buy them or get them from the library?

She I bought them, of course; we have all our books sent from Hatchards.

He Well, that's all right then, isn't it?

She Honestly, I don't think they're worthy of you.

He How do you know?

She Do you – really and truly – like them yourself?

He Tremendously. I just can't put them down.

She Of course, I know they're frightfully clever and all that, but you must admit they don't 'contribute' very much, do they?

He They contribute a hell of a lot to me.

She I wasn't speaking commercially.

He I was.

She With the world in its present state there are so many really important things to write about.

He Name three.

She I know I'm not very good at expressing myself, and I expect you think I'm an awful fool –

He The thought had occurred to me –

She I asked for that – didn't I?

He Yes.

She But a man with your gifts and your experience of the world and people, don't you think you have a sort of responsibility, a sort of duty, to the public?

He In what way?

She You could do so much to help.

He Who?

She All sorts of people.

He How?

She I see it's no use saying any more. You're just deliberately
misunderstanding me.

He I wouldn't be sure of that.

She You must forgive me if I have been impertinent.

He Why?

She I'm sure I'm very sorry if I spoke out of turn. I should have thought a
man in your position would be big enough to be able to take a little
honest criticism.

He Why?

She But I see I was wrong.

He Then you're making giant strides.

South Sea Bubble, 1956

Noël Coward, by Max Beerbohm, 1931

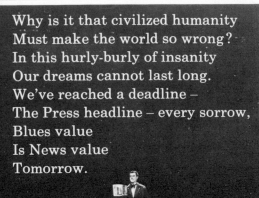

Why is it that civilized humanity
Must make the world so wrong?
In this hurly-burly of insanity
Our dreams cannot last long.
We've reached a deadline –
The Press headline – every sorrow,
Blues value
Is News value
Tomorrow.

Blues,
Twentieth Century Blues,
Are getting me down.
Who's
Escaped those weary
Twentieth Century Blues.
Why,
If there's a God in the sky,
Why shouldn't he grin?
High
Above this dreary
Twentieth Century din,
In this strange illusion,
Chaos and confusion,
People seem to lose their way.
What is there to strive for,
Love or keep alive for? Say –
Hey, hey, call it a day.
Blues,
Nothing to win or to lose.
It's getting me down.
Blues,
I've got those weary
Twentieth Century Blues.

TWENTIETH CENTURY BLUES

Sung by Binnie Barnes in *Cavalcade,* 1931

126

Dance Bar in Baden Baden, 1923, by Max Beckmann
(Günther Franke Collection on loan at Bavarian State Collection, Munich)   127

Dressing Room, 1926, by Walt Kuhn
(The Brooklyn Museum, Gift of Friends of the Museum)

♪ WHY MUST THE SHOW GO ON?

Why must the show go on?
It can't be all that indispensable,
To me it really isn't sensible
On the whole
To play a leading role
While fighting those tears you can't control,
Why kick up your legs
When draining the dregs
Of sorrow's bitter cup?
Because you have read
Some idiot has said
'The Curtain must go up!'
I'd like to know why a star takes bows
Having just returned from burying her spouse.
Brave boop-a-doopers,
Go home and dry your tears,
Gallant old troupers,
You've bored us all for years
And when you're so blue
Wet through
And thoroughly woe-begone,
Why must the show go on?
Oh Mammy!
Why must the show go on?

We're asked to condole
With each tremulous soul
Who steps out to be loudly applauded,
Stars on opening nights
Sob when they see their names in lights,
Though people who act
As a matter of fact
Are financially amply rewarded,
It seems, while pursuing their calling,
Their suffering's simply appalling
But butchers and bakers
And candlestick makers
Get little applause for their pains
And when I think of miners
And waiters in 'Diners'
One query for ever remains:

Why must the show go on?
The rule is surely not immutable,
It might be wiser and more suitable
Just to close

If you are in the throes
Of personal grief and private woes.
Why stifle a sob
When doing your job
When, if you use your head,
You'd go out and grab
A comfortable cab
And go right home to bed?
Because you're not giving us much fun,
This 'Laugh Clown, Laugh' routine's
    been overdone,
Hats off to Show Folks
For smiling when they're blue
But more comme-il-faut folks
Are sick of smiling through,
And if you're out cold
Too old,
And most of your teeth have gone,
Why must the show go on?
I sometimes wonder
Why must the show go on?

Why must the show go on?
Why not announce the closing night of it?
The public seem to hate the sight of it
Dear, and so
Why you should undergo
This terrible strain we'll never know.
We know that you're sad,
We know that you've had
A lot of storm and strife
But is it quite fair
To ask us to share
Your dreary private life?
We know you're trapped in a gilded cage,
But for heaven's sake relax and be your age,
Stop being gallant,
And don't be such a bore,
Pack up your talent,
There's always plenty more.
And if you lose hope
Take dope
And lock yourself in the John,
Why must the show go on?
I'm merely asking
Why must the show go on?

♪ TOURING DAYS

I've often wondered if it's possible to recapture
The magic of bygone days.
I feel that one couldn't quite resuscitate
All the rapture and joy of a youthful phase.
But still it's nice to remember
The things we used to do
When you were on tour with me, my dear
And I was on tour with you.

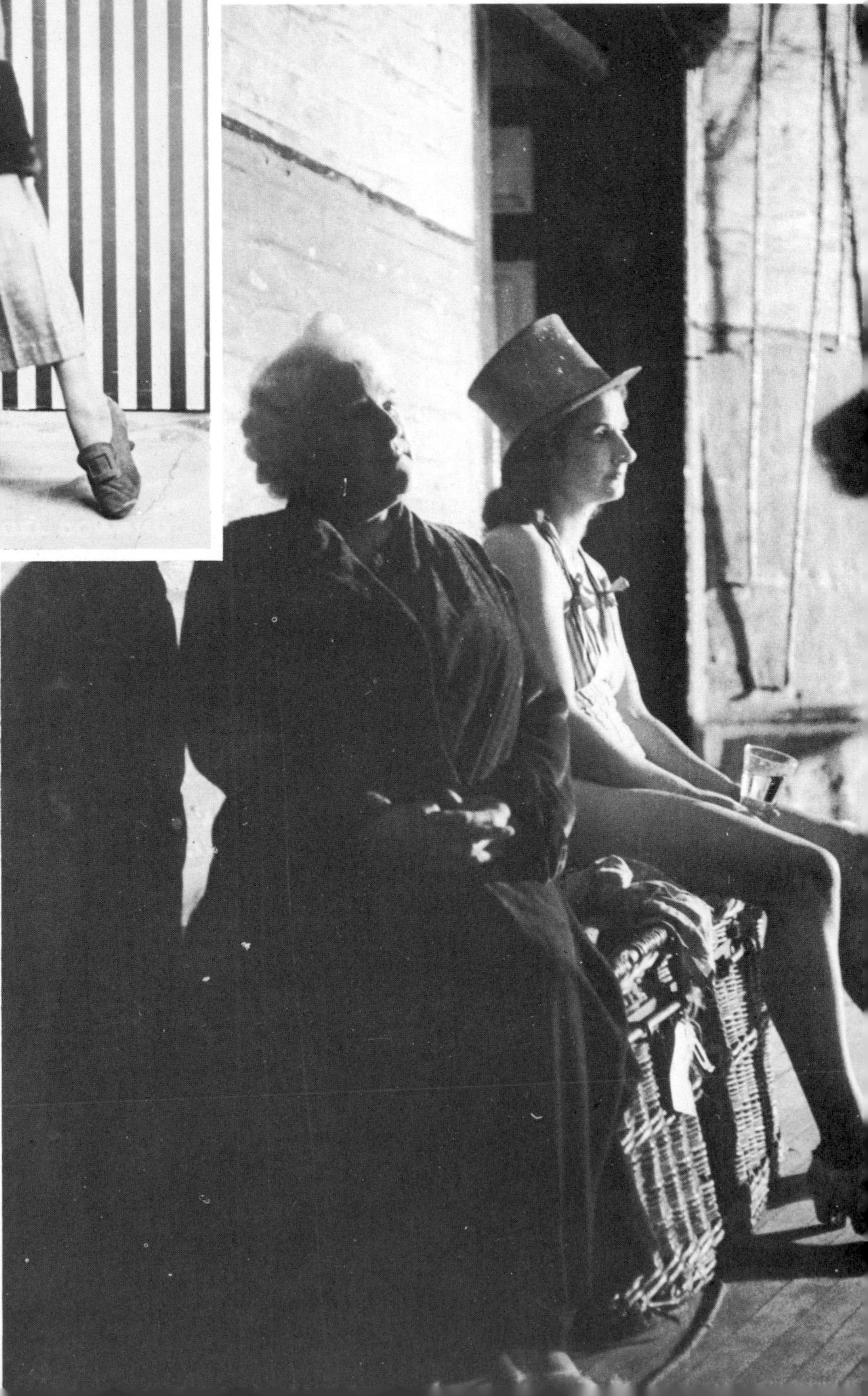

Noël Coward and
Betty Chester,
Birmingham, 1919

132

Touring days, touring days,
What ages it seems to be,
Since the landlady at Norwich
Served a mouse up in the porridge,
And a beetle in the morning tea.
Touring days, alluring days,
Far back in the past we gaze,
We used to tip the dressers every Friday night
And pass it over lightly when they came in tight,
But somehow to us it seemed all right,
Those wonderful touring days.

Collected Sketches and Lyrics, 1931

I'm getting tired of jazz tunes
Monotonous,
They've gotten us
Crazy now.
Though they're amusing as tunes
Music has gone somehow.
I hear the moaning
Groaning
Of a saxophone
  band,

It simply shakes me,
Makes me
Want to play a
Lone hand.
Please understand
I want an age that has tunes
Simple and slow,
I'm feeling so
Lazy now.

TEACH ME TO DANCE

Fox Trot

Black Bottom

Teach me to dance like Grandma used to dance,
I refuse to dance – Blues.
Black Bottoms, Charlestons, what wind blew them in,
Monkeys do them in zoos.
Back in the past the dancing signified
Just a dignified glow.
They didn't have to be so strong
Though they revolved the whole night long.
Teach me to dance like Grandma used to dance
Sixty summers ago!

Sung by Jessie Matthews in
This Year of Grace!, 1928

LIKE GRANDMA

Charleston

'Artistic Valsing'

𝄞 THERE'S A YOUNGER GENERATION KNOCK, KNOCK, KNOCKING AT THE DOOR

Age calls the tune,
Youth's over soon,
That is the natural law.
There's a Younger Generation
Knock knock knocking at the door.
Why sit and fret
Vainly regret
Things that have gone before?
There's a Younger Generation
Knock knock knocking at the door.
Though the world is well lost for love dreams
There's wisdom above dreams
To compensate mothers and wives,
When the days of youth have passed them,
This should last them
All their lives.

I've had my fun,
All that is done,
Why should I sigh for more?
There's a Younger Generation
Knock knock knocking at the door.

Age can be gay,
Age can betray
Destiny's foolish law,
Though the Younger Generation's
Knock knock knocking at the door,
Age is a joke
Planned to provoke
Dreams that the fools ignore,
When the Younger Generation's
Knock knock knocking at the door.

Sung by Rita Lyle in *Words and Music*, 1932

♪ SIGH NO MORE

Sung by Graham Payn in
Sigh No More, 1945

Poor mournful ladies
Are you weeping for a dream
Once dreamed?
Are you still listening for some remembered
Theme
That seemed
To promise happiness and love
  and gentle years
Devoid of fears?
Sweet music starts again
Lift up your hearts again,
And dry, ah, dry those tears.

Sigh no more, sigh no more.
Grey clouds of sorrow fill the sky no more.
Cry no more,
Die no more
Those little deaths at parting,
New life and new love are starting,
Sing again, sing again,
The Winter's over and it's Spring again.
Joy is your
Troubadour,
Sweet and beguiling ladies, sigh no more,
Sigh no more,
Sweet and beguiling ladies, sigh no more.

♪ COME THE WILD WILD WEATHER

Come the wild, wild weather,
Come the wind, come the rain,
Come the little white flakes of snow,
Come the joy, come the pain,
We shall still be together
When our life's journey ends,
For wherever we chance to go
We shall always be friends.
We may find while we're travelling through the years
Moments of joy and love and happiness,
Reason for grief, reason for tears.
Come the wild, wild weather,
If we've lost or we've won,
We'll remember these words we say,
Till our story is done.

Sung by Graham Payn in
Waiting in the Wings, 1960

Nothing can last for ever,
Settle for now or never,
Waste no regrets
On moments that are past,
Nothing can ever last.

Sung by Sylvia Cecil in
Ace of Clubs, 1950

Sir Noël Coward, by Derek Hill

CURTAIN CALL

When I was one and twenty I was ambitious, cheerful, and high-spirited . . . and was briskly unaware that I belonged to a dying civilization. Today this dubious implication is pitched at me from all directions. Despair is the new religion, the new mode; it is in the books we read, the music we hear, and, very much too often, it is in the plays we see. Well, I am no longer one and twenty . . . I am still ambitious and cheerful, and not offensively high-spirited and still unaware that I belong to a dying civilization. If I do, there really isn't anything I can do about it and so I shall just press on with my life as I like living it until I die of natural causes or an H-Bomb blows me to smithereens. I knew, in my teens, that the world was full of hatred, envy, malice, cruelty, jealousy, unrequited love, murder, despair and destruction. I also knew, at the same time, that it was full of kindness, joy, pleasure, requited love, generosity, fun, excitement, laughter and friends. Nothing that has happened to me over the years has caused me to re-adjust in my mind the balance of these observed phenomena.

Future Indefinite, 1954

I'll follow my secret heart
My whole life through,
I'll keep all my dreams apart
Till one comes true.
No matter what price is paid,
What stars may fade
Above,
I'll follow my secret heart
Till I find love.

Sung by the Author
and Yvonne Printemps in
Conversation Piece, 1934

Sung by Peggy Wood and George Metaxa in
Bitter Sweet, 1929

I'll see you again,
Whenever Spring breaks through again;
Time may lie heavy between,
But what has been
Is past forgetting.

This sweet memory,
Across the years will come to me;
Though my world may go awry,
In my heart will ever lie
Just the echo of a sigh,
Goodbye.

Sources of Illustrations

In this list the following abbreviations have been used: Barnaby's Picture Library – Barnaby's; Conway Picture Library – Conway; Fox Photos Ltd – Fox; Keystone Press Agency Ltd – Keystone; Raymond Mander & Joe Mitchenson Theatre Collection – M & M; The Mansell Collection – Mansell; Paul Popper Ltd – Popper; Radio Times Hulton Picture Library – RTH.

Acknowledgments

SIGH NO MORE.
(Nina, I Wonder What Happened to Him, Sigh No More Ladies.)
Copyright © Chappell & Co. Ltd, London, 1945, and Chappell & Co. Inc. U.S.A. Copyright renewed.

ACE OF CLUBS.
(In a Boat On a Lake, I Like America, Nothing Can Last for Ever.)
Copyright © Chappell & Co. Ltd, London, 1950, and Chappell & Co. Inc. U.S.A.

ALL CLEAR (SET TO MUSIC).
(I've Been to a Marvellous Party.)
Copyright © Chappell & Co. Ltd, London, 1939, and Chappell & Co. Inc. U.S.A. Copyright renewed.

WORDS AND MUSIC.
(Younger Generation, Mad About the Boy.)
Copyright © Chappell & Co. Ltd, London, 1932, and Chappell & Co. Inc. U.S.A. Copyrights renewed.

CAVALCADE. (Twentieth Century Blues.)
Copyright © Chappell & Co. Ltd, London, 1931, and Chappell & Co. Inc. U.S.A. Copyright renewed.

ON WITH THE DANCE. (Poor Little Rich Girl.)
Copyright © Ascherberg, Hopwood & Crew Ltd, London, 1925, and Warner Bros. Music U.S.A. Copyright renewed.

WAITING IN THE WINGS. (Come the Wild Wild Weather.)
Copyright © Chappell & Co. Ltd, London, 1960, and Chappell & Co. Inc. U.S.A.

THE GLOBE REVUE.
(There Are Bad Times Just Around the Corner.)
Copyright © Chappell & Co. Ltd, London, 1952, and Chappell & Co. Inc. U.S.A.

LONDON CALLING. (Parisian Pierrot.)
Copyright © Keith Prowse Music Co. Ltd, 1923. Copyright renewed.

Don't Put Your Daughter On the Stage Mrs. Worthington.
Copyright © Chappell & Co. Ltd, London, 1935, and Chappell & Co. Inc. U.S.A. Copyright renewed.

Let's Do It. (Sir Noel Coward's lyric to Cole Porter's song.)
Copyright © Chappell & Co. Ltd, London, 1928, and Warner Bros. Music U.S.A. Copyright renewed.

London Pride.
Copyright © Chappell & Co. Ltd, London, 1941, and Chappell & Co. Inc. U.S.A. Copyright renewed.

Mad Dogs and Englishmen.
Copyright © Chappell & Co. Ltd, London, 1932, and Warner Bros. Music U.S.A. Copyright renewed.

Why Must the Show Go On?
Copyright © Chappell & Co. Ltd, London, 1957, and Chappell & Co. Inc. U.S.A.

Alice Is At It Again.
Copyright © Chappell & Co. Ltd, London, 1955, and Chappell & Co. Inc. U.S.A.

Could You Please Oblige Us With a Bren Gun?
Copyright © Chappell & Co. Ltd, London, 1941, and Chappell & Co. Inc. U.S.A. Copyright renewed.

Louisa.
Copyright © Chappell & Co. Ltd, London, 1965, and Chappell & Co. Inc. U.S.A.

Touring Days.
Copyright © Chappell & Co. Ltd, London, 1973.

NOT YET THE DODO. (The Boy Actor.)
Copyright © Noël Coward, 1967. Published by Wm Heinemann Ltd, London, and Doubleday & Company Inc.

PRESENT INDICATIVE.
(Personal Reminiscence, New York 1921, Magic of an Empty Theatre, Auditions, Success.)
Copyright © Noël Coward, 1937. Published by Wm Heinemann Ltd, London, and Doubleday & Co. Inc. Copyright renewed.

PRESENT LAUGHTER. (Penalty of Success.)
Copyright © Noël Coward, 1943. Published by Wm Heinemann Ltd, London, and Doubleday & Co. Inc. Copyright renewed.

TONIGHT AT EIGHT-THIRTY: SHADOW PLAY.
(Shadow Play.)
Copyright © Noël Coward, 1936. Published by Wm Heinemann Ltd, London, and Doubleday & Co. Inc. Copyright renewed.

QUADRILLE. (The New World.)
Copyright © Noël Coward, 1952. Published by Wm Heinemann Ltd, London, and Doubleday & Company Inc.

FUTURE INDEFINITE. (Return to London.)
Copyright © Noël Coward, 1954. Published by Wm Heinemann Ltd, London, and Doubleday & Company Inc.

SOUTH SEA BUBBLE. (Last Words.)
Copyright © Noël Coward, 1956. Published by Wm Heinemann Ltd, London

TONIGHT AT EIGHT-THIRTY: SHADOW PLAY.
(You Were There, Play Orchestra Play.)
Copyright © Chappell & Co. Ltd, London, 1935, and Chappell & Co., Inc. U.S.A. Copyrights renewed.

THIS YEAR OF GRACE!
(A Room With a View, Try to Learn to Love, Dance Little Lady, Teach Me to Dance Like Grandma.)
Copyright © Chappell & Co. Ltd, London, 1928, and Chappell & Co. Inc. U.S.A. Copyright renewed.

COCHRAN'S 1931 REVUE. (Any Little Fish.)
Copyright © Chappell & Co. Ltd, London, 1931, and Warner Bros. Music U.S.A. Copyright renewed.

SAIL AWAY.
(Why Do the Wrong People Travel?
Useless Useful Phrases, When You Want Me, Beatnik Love Affair, Bronxville Darby and Joan, The Passenger's Always Right.)
Copyright © Noël Coward, 1950. Published by Chappell & Co. Ltd, London, and Chappell & Co. Inc. U.S.A.

OPERETTE. (Dearest Love, The Stately Homes of England.)
Copyright © Chappell & Co. Ltd, London, 1938, and Chappell & Co. Inc. U.S.A. Copyrights renewed.

THE GIRL WHO CAME TO SUPPER.
(Saturday Night at the Rose and Crown, London is a Little Bit Bit of All Right, What Ho Mrs Brisket, Don't Take Our Charlie for the Army)
Copyright © Noël Coward, 1963. Published by Chappell & Co. Ltd, London, and Chappell & Co. Inc. U.S.A.

AFTER THE BALL. (London at Night.)
Copyright © Chappell & Co. Ltd, London, 1954, and Chappell & Co. Inc. U.S.A.

BITTER-SWEET. (I'll See You Again, If Love Were All.)
Copyright © Chappell & Co. Ltd, London, 1929, and Warner Bros. Music U.S.A. Copyrights renewed.

CONVERSATION PIECE (I'll Follow My Secret Heart.)
Copyright © Chappell & Co. Ltd, London, 1934, and Chappell & Co. Inc. U.S.A. Copyright renewed.

Index of Lyrics and Verses